Greetings from
Fort Myers & Sanibel Island

Donald D. Spencer

Schiffer Publishing Ltd®

4880 Lower Valley Road, Atglen, Pennsylvania 19310

Dedication

To my daughter, Sherrie Rae Spencer

Photo Credits
Dover Publications Inc. (pages 9 (right), 10 (left), 90) and photographs from the Florida State Photographic Archives (pages 14 (left), 39 (top), 40 (top), 73 (top left), 86 (left), 87 (top right), and 88, 89 (bottom left)).

Designed by Stephanie Daugherty
Type set in MisterEarl Bd BT/MisterEarl Lt BT /Swis721 Lt BT/
ISBN: 978-0-7643-3305-7
Printed in China

Other Schiffer Books by Donald D. Spencer:

Greetings from Sarasota, Bradentown, & Surrounding Communities
978-0-7643-3213-5, $24.99

Greetings from St. Augustine
978-0-7643-2802-2, $24.95

Greetings from Tampa
978-0-7643-2898-5, $24.95

Greetings from Jacksonville, Florida
978-0-7643-2958-6, $24.99

Other Schiffer Books on Related Subjects:

Greetings from St. Petersburg
978-0-7643-2690-5, $24.95

Miami Beach Postcards
0-7643-2306-7, $14.95

South Beach Postcards
978-0-7643-2630-1, $8.95

Schiffer Books are available at special discounts for bulk purchases for sales promotions or premiums. Special editions, including personalized covers, corporate imprints, and excerpts can be created in large quantities for special needs. For more information contact the publisher:

Schiffer Publishing Ltd.
4880 Lower Valley Road
Atglen, PA 19310
Phone: (610) 593-1777; Fax: (610) 593-2002
E-mail: Info@schifferbooks.com

For the largest selection of fine reference books on this and related subjects, please visit our web site at:

www.schifferbooks.com

We are always looking for people to write books on new and related subjects. If you have an idea for a book please contact us at the above address.

This book may be purchased from the publisher. Include $5.00 for shipping. Please try your bookstore first. You may write for a free catalog.

In Europe, Schiffer books are distributed by
Bushwood Books
6 Marksbury Ave.
Kew Gardens
Surrey TW9 4JF England
Phone: 44 (0) 20 8392 8585; Fax: 44 (0) 20 8392 9876
E-mail: info@bushwoodbooks.co.uk
Website: www.bushwoodbooks.co.uk

Contents

4

Preface: Postcards and People

Hand painted in soft colors, postmarks still visible, old postcards offer views of scenes both familiar and removed. They evoke memories of a happy time gone by, and, like family photographs, they remind us of what's changed.

A postcard is better than a thousand words. The cards depict everything from downtown street scenes, to buildings that no longer stand, to neighborhoods, to parks, to tourist attractions such as the beaches. Though often faded, many still have original handwritten messages on them. The backs of postcards are often more interesting than the fronts because they share a moment from people's lives. A poignant message and the date and place from where the card was sent add interest for some collectors.

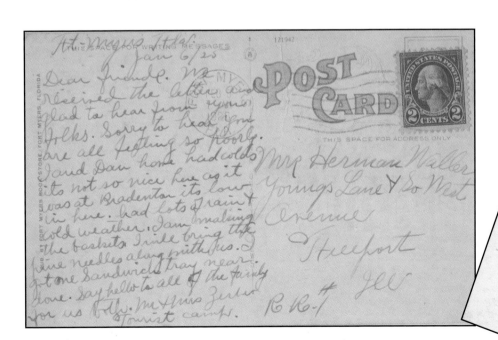

A History of the Postcard

Early Postcards

Postcards first appeared in Austria in 1869 and in England and France in 1870. These early European cards carried no images; only space on one side for an address, the reverse side was for a message. But they enjoyed an advantage over first-class letter mail; they could be mailed at a reduced rate of postage. The first picture postcards appeared in Germany in 1870. The United States began to issue picture postcards in 1873 in conjunction with the Columbian Exposition in Chicago. These were illustrations on government printed postal cards and on privately printed souvenir cards. On May 19, 1898, private printers were granted permission, by an act of congress, to print and sell cards that bore the inscription "Private Mailing Card." The government granted the use of the word POST CARD to private printers on December 4, 1901. As a result, private citizens began to take black and white photographs and have them printed on paper with postcard backs. These cards are commonly called Real Photo postcards.

Real Photo Postcards

In 1902, Eastman Kodak marketed its postcard size photographic papers. They quickly followed with a folding camera (model No. 3A) that was specially designed for making Real Photo postcards. To make matters even simpler, an amateur photographer could mail the camera with exposed film to Eastman Kodak. They would develop and print the postcards and return them to the sender with a reloaded

camera. These innovations in photography as applied to the postcard captured the public's imagination. It had become possible for anyone who owned a camera to make personalized photo postcards.

Postcards Become Popular

The picture postcard did not come into common use in the United States until after 1900. It was about 1902 that the postcard craze hit the country and it was not long before a wide variety of printed postcards were available: advertising, expositions, political, greetings, and more. Collectors would send postcards to total strangers in faraway places, asking for local cards in return. Some collectors specialized in railroad depots, street scenes, cemeteries, churches, courthouses, farms, holidays, animals, military scenes, casinos, ethnic images, sports, hotels, transportation, parks, bathing beauties, industrial scenes, beach scenes, plants, lighthouses, restaurants, space, amusement parks, rivers, steamboats, plants, agricultural products, even comic cards; others collected anything they could find. Postcard albums, bought by the millions, were filled with every sort of postcard ever issued. The craze was actually worldwide since many countries had postcards. Acceptance by the public was immediate and enthusiastic. Postcards afforded an easy means of communication. They were an early version of today's email, though slower, of course, relying as they did on mail service.

Divided Back Postcards

Before March 1, 1907, it was illegal to write any message on the same side of the card as the address. For that reason the early postcards often have handwriting all over the sides of the picture, and sometimes right across it. Many an otherwise beautiful card was defaced in this way. When postcards first started to go through the mail, they were postmarked at the receiving post office as well as that of the sender, making it easy to see the time involved between post offices—sometimes remarkably brief! The volume of postcards was an important reason for discontinuing the unnecessary second marking about 1910. For years postcards cost only a nickel for six and the postage was a penny, right up to World War II.

The most popular American postcards up to World War I were those made in Germany from photographs supplied by American publishers. At the time of the postcard craze, of course, color photography was still something of a rarity and not commercially viable. For the color cards, black and white photos were touched up, hand-colored, and then generally reproduced by lithography. Lithography consists of transferring the image to a lithographic stone, offset to a rubber blanket, and then printed onto paper. The details in the German produced cards were extremely sharp, and the best of them technically have never been matched since.

Large Letter Postcard
The large letter postcard is probably the most popular postcard of the twentieth century. Though not quite a view card and not quite a greeting card, the large letter card communicated "postcard" to anyone who sees the image. Although large letter designs go back to the Golden Age of Postcards, it is during the linen era (1930s-1940s) that large letters, with their bold colors, graphics and type faces secured their status as icons of Americans. The large letter "Greetings from" state and city postcards are the colorful reminders of each state or city a traveler has visited. The cards combine flora and fauna with points of interest into collages that celebrate the unique character of each state or city, such as a military base or roadside attraction. In 2002, the United States Postal System issued a set of "Greetings from America" postage stamps that portrayed large letter postcards of the fifty states. *Circa 1930s-1940s, $3-5.*

Linen Postcards

In 1930, the "linen" textured card was introduced and was popular until 1950. While this card was less expensive to produce, it reduced the clarity of detail in the pictures. These cheap cards are typically printed in vivid colors on paper with a crosshatched surface, which resembled linen fabric. "Linen" refers to the texture-like feel of the cardboard stock. The cards of this period romanticized the images of diners, gas stations, hotels, commercial buildings, and tourist attractions. Using the photographic image of an establishment, all undesirable features, such as background clutter, people, telephone poles, and even cars were removed by airbrushing. World War II occupied most people's attention during much of this period, but the prosperity that followed was reflected in cards from communities all over the United States.

Photochrome Postcards

In 1950, the "photochrome" or "chrome" postcard with a glossy finish replaced the linen card. This type of finish allowed for a very sharp reproduction of the picture, however, the cards lost much of both the role and nature of earlier cards. The chrome card, which is offered for sale today in gift shops, is where full-color photographic images are reproduced as a half-tone on modern lithography presses. A varnish or lamination is applied on the card to give it a shiny look. In 1970, a king-sized chrome card (4.125" by 5.875") was introduced, and by 1978, it was in general use everywhere. This card is also called a continental or modern postcard.

The German postcard industry folded in the summer of 1914, when the war struck Europe, and never revived. Postcards produced during the years 1907 and 1915 had a divided back: the address was to be written on the right side; the left side was for writing messages. Millions of postcards were published during these years. Postcard collectors have hailed these opening years of the twentieth century as the "Golden Age" of postcards. During the golden era of the picture postcard, billions of postcards rolled off the printing presses. In 1917 the United States entered World War I and the postcard craze ended.

White Border Postcards

With the advent of World War I, the supply of postcards for American consumption switched from Germany to England and the United States. Postcards printed in the United States during the years 1915-1930 were classified as White Border cards. To save ink, a colorless border was left around the view. These postcards were of a poorer quality as compared to the cards printed in Germany.

Florida's Early Years

Through the years colorful characters have populated, explored, and plundered the land, but the legends have hung on and the people have preserved South Florida. Indigenous people migrated to the lower peninsula at least 11,000 years ago; Spanish explorer Juan Ponce de Leon, who founded Florida, died from a native Calusa Indian's arrow; and the pirate Black Caesar ambushed sailing ships passing his refuge at present day Caesars Creek. Local folklore recounts tales of his buried treasure, cruelty, and daring raids.

Southwest Florida was shaped and reshaped by centuries of flooding during the Ice Ages. Each time the polar ice sheets reformed and lowered the surrounding sea level, another layer of sand and shell was deposited, creating the limestone and sandy sediment that underlies much of the area today. The southern tip of Florida was last submerged about 25,000 years ago.

Today the subtropical areas around Fort Myers and south to Naples are having a new era of sustained growth in tourism, agriculture, business, and real estate. It is one of the fastest developing areas in the nation.

The American Serengeti

Rich fossil finds show that this region was once home to camels, mastodons, mammoths, and wild horses. The animal population reached its peak during the

Pleistocene Period about 10,000 years ago, when the number and variety of animals here approached that of the big game region of the African Serengeti. Gradual changes in climate and vegetation contributed to their extinction.

The first humans reached Southwest Florida at least 10,000 years ago when the climate was colder and drier. Living in small, widely scattered bands, these first Floridians, or Paleo Indians, survived by hunting, fishing, and gathering wild plant foods.

Exotic Land Animals.
Southwest Florida was once home to some of the most exotic and remarkable land animals that ever lived: elephant-like mammoths and mastodons, herds of camel, horses, and long-horned bison, fierce saber cats with nine-inch fangs, lions, and huge armadillos, crocodiles, land tortoises, rhinoceroses, vicious wolves up to seven feet long, giant ground sloths that could graze on treetops twenty feet high, and short-faced bears that grew to nearly twice the size of a modern day grizzly.

Calusa Indian Society.

Centuries before Columbus set foot in the Americas, a powerful and highly-developed Indian civilization was flourishing along the islands and grassy marshes of Southwest Florida's Gulf Coast. Once numbering as many as 10,000, these direct descendants of Florida's early mastodon hunters were given the name Calusa by the first Spanish explorers—a native word they understood to mean "fierce and warlike." By the beginning of the sixteenth century, the Calusas controlled the southern half of Florida from the Gulf of Mexico to Lake Okeechobee. This vast empire dominated some fifty towns and villages and stretched inland through the Everglades for hundreds of miles. This view appears at the Museum of Florida History in Tallahassee.

Calusa Indians

Centuries before Columbus, Florida's lower Gulf Coast was controlled by the powerful Calusa Indians. Once numbering as many as 10,000, the Calusa were ruled by a single chief and he was supported by a nobility and strong military force. They dug canals, built huge mounds of shell and earth for their temples, and collected tribute from towns and villages throughout Southwest Florida. Highly skilled artisans carved elaborate masks and objects for religious and ceremonial purposes. Although the tribe is now extinct, ceremonial, burial, and refuse shell mounds are found on several islands including Mound Key, Pine, Sanibel, and Useppa.

Florida's First Tourist

Juan Ponce de Leon, who discovered and claimed Florida for Spain in 1513, led the first recorded European exploration of the Gulf Coast.

Paleo Indians—Florida's First People.

The first humans drifted into Southwest Florida at least 10,000 years ago while much of North America was still covered by massive ice sheets. Living in small, widely scattered bands, these first Floridians, or Paleo Indians, discovered a hunter's paradise with abundant game and dry, mild winters. The Paleo Indians survived by hunting mammoths, mastodons, and a wide variety of smaller animals. They were almost constantly on the move, following close behind the migrating herds and making their temporary camps near freshwater springs and rivers.

Florida Discovered By Ponce de Leon.

In 1512, the King of Spain granted Juan Ponce de Leon a patent to discover and settle the island of Bimini. At his own expense, he outfitted three vessels—the *Santa Maria,* the *Santiago,* and the *San Cristobai*—for the expedition and set out with a crew of about two hundred men. Sailing in the spring of 1513, he cruised among the Bahamas Islands hoping to find Bimini. Instead he sighted land northwest of the Bahamas. On March 27, Ponce claimed the land for Spain and named it Florida. After returning to Spain in 1514, he returned to Florida in 1521 to try and establish a permanent colony in Southwest Florida, but the hostile Calusa Indians drove the Spaniards back to their ships. Ponce received an arrow wound that proved fatal; he died in 1521 and was later buried in Puerto Rico.

Calusa Indian Family.

The Calusa Indians were "city dwellers" whose sea-oriented high, dry, airy rectangular dwelling mounds made pleasant and secure home sites. Skillful engineers, they surrounded their terraced mounds with kitchen garden courts; waterways and boat basins; ramps, causeways, and ponds where live fish and shellfish were stored. Shell-paved causeways and canals led from the living city to mound cities for the dead and to other "midden" mounds where waste was discarded. The tallest mounds held temples, store houses, and homes of their leaders. The Calusa Indians were also connected to other Indian peoples throughout eastern North America. Ancient trade networks supplied the Calusas with exotic materials in exchange for large seashells and other local goods. This view of a Calusa Indian family and their home atop a shell midden appears as part of a Calusa Indian exhibit at the Florida Museum of Natural History in Gainesville.

He returned to colonize Southwest Florida in 1521, but was mortally wounded by a Calusa Indian arrow. Other Spanish explorers attempted the conquest of Florida over the next forty years. The expeditions failed, but decades of warfare, enslavement, and runaway epidemics of European diseases destroyed the Calusas and their culture.

In 1565, Spanish conquistador Pedro Menendez, the founder of St. Augustine, sailed to Southwest Florida to make peace with the native Calusa Indians and settle the land for his king. His fleet was caught in a storm and the crew took refuge in a Tequesta Indian village in Biscayne Bay.

Menendez returned in 1567, and it was during this voyage that he established a mission, which was protected by thirty soldiers. The Spanish soldiers occasionally would provoke acts of hostility and one such incident culminated in the killing of one of the uncles of the Tequesta chief. This enraged the Tequestas — they attacked and forced the missionaries to retreat.

The Spanish continued to establish missions and forts along the Florida coast in an effort to strengthen their hold on the New World. During this time, however, the Tequesta and Calusa Indians began to feel the decimating effects of slave raids and European diseases. By the late eighteenth century, the native populations of Southwest Florida were reduced to a handful of survivors.

However, by the early 1700s, small bands of Creek Indians from Georgia and Alabama began making their way into Florida. Eventually, these breakaway groups of Indians joined with escaped black slaves and refugees from other tribes to forge a new identity known as the Seminole. Ongoing disputes and skirmishes with white settlers eventually led to government pressure to move the Seminoles to reservations west of the Mississippi River.

Seminole Indians.
Seminole Indians poling their dugout canoes in the Everglades. *Circa 1915, $4-6.*

Gulf Coast Pirates

Legend has it that Spanish pirate Jose Gaspar (Gasparilla) made his home in the islands just west of Fort Myers, reportedly establishing headquarters on Sanibel Island, holding his female prisoners captive on Captiva Island, burying his booty on Gasparilla Island, and imprisoning his beloved Mexican Princess Joseffa on Useppa Island. He drowned himself in anchor chains in 1821 about the time the United States bought Florida from Spain.

Gulf Coast Pirates.
Pirates attack ships and ports, stealing treasure and other goods. The Gulf Coast of Florida was a pirate stronghold.

Florida Becomes An American Possession

Spain was unable to control the Indians and rule her territory. Finally, after much discussion, a treaty was signed in which Spain agreed to transfer Florida to the United States for the sum of five million dollars. The exchange of flags took place July 10, 1821, at St. Augustine (capital of East Florida), and July 17, 1821, at Pensacola (capital of West Florida). After more than three hundred years of Spanish and British rule, Florida became part of the United States.

In 1822, the United States made Florida a Territory and began preparing it for statehood.

In 1838, Floridians held a convention for the purpose of writing a constitution, or a set of laws, by which the state would be governed. Fifty-six people from all parts of the territory took part in this convention. Florida voters approved the constitution in 1839 and six years later Florida became the twenty-seventh state in the United States.

THE CHANGE OF FLAGS~JULY 10TH 1821

Florida Becomes Part of America.
Florida came into American hands through a treaty signed with Spain in 1821. On July 10, the Spanish flag came down for the last time, and the starred flag of the United States rose over Castillo de San Marcos, shown in the background. *Circa 1940s, $6-8.*

The Seminole Wars.
Three conflicts between the United States and the Seminole Indians of Florida resulted in freeing this desirable Indian land for white exploration and settlement: First Seminole War (1817-1818), Second Seminole War (1835-1842), and Third Seminole War (1855-1858). The wars were brought on by U.S. territorial expansion, native factions resisting the U.S. policy of removal, and slavery. There was constant turmoil on the Florida border. Slaves seeking freedom slipped across from Alabama and Georgia, and parties of slave catchers roved in Spanish North Florida. The Spanish government could not maintain order. At the end of the Third Seminole War in 1858, the remaining Seminole Indians either migrated to present day Oklahoma with their leader Billy Bowlegs, or remained behind in the Florida Everglades area. Descendants of the remaining Seminoles still live in Florida and claim the rights of a sovereign nation. This is a scene from a Seminole War reenactment. *Author photograph.*

Civil War.
During the Civil War (1861-1865), Union forces occupied many coastal towns and forts while the interior of the state remained in Confederate hands. Florida provided an estimated 15,000 troops and a significant amount of supplies to the Confederacy including salt, beef, port, and cotton. Tallahassee was the only southern capital east of the Mississippi River to avoid capture during the war, spared by southern victories at Olustee (1864) and Natural Bridge (1865). This scene is from a Florida Civil War reenactment. *Author photograph.*

The Seminole Wars

The three Seminole Indian wars were brought on by U.S. territorial expansion, native factions resisting the U.S. policy of removal, and slavery. There was constant turmoil on the Florida border as slaves seeking freedom slipped across from Georgia and Alabama. Parties of slave catchers roved in Spanish North Florida and the Spanish government could not maintain order.

During the Seminole Wars of 1817-1818 (First Seminole War) and 1835-1842 (Second Seminole War), Florida became saturated with forts, camps, stockades, and blockhouses of all descriptions. During this period more than eighty forts—including Fort Myers—were in use throughout Florida.

Civil War (1861-1865)

The Civil War was a period of internal conflict for the United States. In 1861, Florida seceded from the Union and joined the newly formed country, the Confederate States of America. That same year the Civil War began between the United States of America and the Confederate States of America. The war between the North and South lasted four long years. It was the most tragic war in American history. More Americans died in the War Between the States than in all wars of the United States combined, until the Vietnam War.

Life on the Florida Frontier

Southwest Florida remained virtually uninhabited until after the Civil War, when handfuls of farmers and squatters began making their way south in mule wagons, ox carts, and sailboats.

Early pioneers fished and hunted for a living, raised crops of cabbage, peppers, tomatoes, and pineapples, dug clams, made charcoal, sold bird plumes, and trapped otters and alligators for their pelts and hides. By the late 1880s, Fort Myers and Naples were already gaining popularity as winter resorts for wealthy Northerners and sportsmen.

Bird Slaughtering

By the turn of the twentieth century South Florida had become home to poachers and plume hunters. Plumes of great and snowy egrets were in demand as fashion accessories. Hunters slaughtered these wading birds by the thousands for their colorful feathers, and several species came dangerously close to extinction. By 1906 public outrage and the demand for protecting the wading birds led to the establishment of protected areas in several State Parks. On December 6, 1947, President Harry S. Truman dedicated the Everglades National Park, which protected not only the birds, but also the alligators and other wild animals. Today, Everglades National Park is a wetland of international importance, as well as a World Heritage Site and International Biosphere Reserve.

Cattle Ranching.
It may not be the common image of Florida, but there is a strong cattle industry in the state and Lee County is part of it. Florida became the second biggest producer east of the Mississippi River and ninth overall for beef cattle numbers. Brahma cattle were used to add size, hardiness, and resistance to heat and insects. They were first brought to Florida in the 1850s. *Author photograph.*

The Tropical Range

Cattle ranching is one of Southwest Florida's oldest industries. By the early 1900s many ranchers were grazing herds of scrub cattle on the open prairies around Immokalee and east of Fort Myers. Railroads improved the access to market in the 1920s and helped raise the area's cattle industry to national importance by the end of World War II.

Flexible Gunnery School.
During World War II the Flexible Gunnery School was located at the Buckingham Army Air Field, east of Fort Myer in Buckingham. Here thousands of military personnel were trained on turret and waist guns on Army Air Force bombers. *Circa 1940s, $3-5.*

World War II.
Florida provided extensive training facilities and more than 250,000 service personnel during World War II; travel restrictions during the war almost destroyed Florida's tourist industry. Shown are military personnel loading bombs on Flying Fortress at MacDill Field, north of Fort Myers. *Circa 1940s, $4-6.*

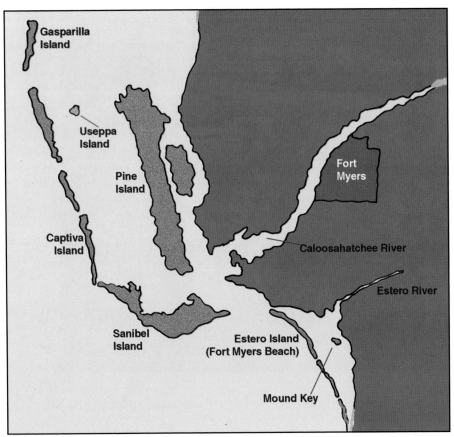

Only Yesterday

World War II introduced hundreds of servicemen to Southwest Florida when Gunnery School and Coast Guard facilities were activated in Fort Myers, and an Army Air Field was established in Naples to train combat pilots. Many veterans returned after the war as prospective homebuyers and businessmen.

Gulf Islands

Around Fort Myers

In the area west of Fort Myers are the islands of Sanibel, Captiva, Estero, Pine, Gasparilla, Mound Key, and Useppa. All the islands are accessible by automobile except for Mound Key and Useppa, which are smaller islands located near Fort Myers. The only way to visit and understand these islands is by private boat or to go on a tour with a charter boat service.

All these islands have a fascinating early history. The clever, powerful Calusa Indians thrived on the Gulf Islands for at least 1,500 years. There were more than fifty Indian villages near present-day Fort Myers. The blue-green waters of Southwest Florida's estuaries—places where fresh water from the land meets and mixes with salt water of the ocean—provided the Indians with such an abundance that they thrived for many centuries without ever needing to farm.

Sanibel and Captiva Islands are known worldwide as two of the premier shelling beach areas. Throughout the 1950s and 1960s, Sanibel and Captiva's reputation as sanctuary islands attracted more and more visitors who arrived via a half-hour ferry ride from the mainland. In 1963, the Sanibel Causeway opened, which allowed visitors to drive their automobiles to the islands.

Map of the Gulf Islands around Fort Myers.
Artist's conception of the Gulf Islands: Captiva Island, Estero Island (Fort Myers Beach), Gasparilla Island, Mound Key, Pine Island, Sanibel Island, and Useppa Island.

Part I: Fort Myers

Looking Up Orange River at Sunset, Fort Myers, Florida

· Robertson and Fresh

Fort Myers is situated on the Caloosahatchee River, a few miles from the Gulf of Mexico, on the west coast of Florida, about 147 miles south of Tampa and 143 miles due west from Palm Beach. It is 442 miles farther south than San Diego, California and almost due south of Cleveland, Ohio.

Chapter One:
Welcome to Fort Myers

The Beginning

Fort Myers began as a military fort, being one of the first forts built along the Caloosahatchee River as a base of operations against the Seminole Indians. Fort Denaud, Fort Thompson, and Fort Dulany (Punta Rassa) all pre-dated Fort Myers. After a hurricane destroyed Fort Dulany in 1841, the military was forced to look for a site less exposed to storms from the Gulf of Mexico. As a result, Fort Harvie was built on the ground that now comprises downtown Fort Myers.

Renewed war against the Seminole Indians in 1850 caused a re-occupation and extensive reconstruction of Fort Harvie. The post was then renamed Fort Myers in honor of Colonel Abraham E. Myers, who was soon to wed the daughter of Major General David E. Twiggs, then commanding Fort Brooke (Tampa). The expanded fort eventually became quite an impressive base. At its peak, it featured a 1,000-foot wharf and more than fifty buildings constructed of hardy yellow pine. The cleared ground around the fort fell roughly within the area bounded by the present-day streets of Hough, Monroe, and Second. The garrison protected settlers in the surrounding area, and a small community grew around the fort.

Born in Georgetown, South Carolina, on May 11, 1811, Abraham Charles Myers was the son of a lawyer and mayor of the city. His father educated him for a military career and Abraham graduated from West Point in 1833. He participated in the Second Seminole War (1835-1842) and in the Mexican War (1846-1848) where he won honorary promotions from Lieutenant to Lieutenant Colonel. For a brief period, he was Quartermaster of the entire army in Mexico. When General David E. Twiggs became commanding officer of the army in Florida, he brought with him his Quartermaster, Lieutenant Colonel Myers.

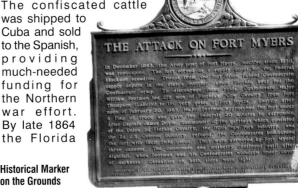

Greetings from Fort Myers.
Fort Myers, the hub city of tropical Lee County, is known as the "City of Palms." It's a place with much history—the fort was headquarters for those pioneers who fought the Seminole Indian Wars in the mid-1800s. During the War Between the States, Fort Myers was activated as a base to round up wild cattle to supply beef to Federal gunboats patrolling the Gulf off Sanibel Island. *Circa 1930s, $3-5.*

Fort Myers Guardhouse.
Fort Myers was constructed in 1850 on the same site as the much smaller Fort Harvie, which had been built in 1841. The Third Seminole War swirled around Fort Myers from 1855 to 1858. After Billy Bowlegs, a Seminole Indian leader, surrendered to the Army in Fort Myers, the fort was abandoned. It was reoccupied six years later in 1864 during the Civil War. After the fort was no longer used by the military, the site became the downtown area of the city of Fort Myers. Shown is a sketch of a Fort Myers guardhouse that appeared in the October 2, 1856 issue of *Frank Leslie's Illustrated Newspaper.*

The Attack on Fort Myers

Fort Myers would once again see service near the end of the Civil War. Though not of strategic significance, by the end of the war, Florida had become a major supplier of cattle to the Confederate Armies. Union forces re-established Fort Myers in 1864 to stage raids on the Florida cattle industry. The confiscated cattle was shipped to Cuba and sold to the Spanish, providing much-needed funding for the Northern war effort. By late 1864 the Florida

Historical Marker on the Grounds of the Southwest Florida Museum of History. *Author photograph.*

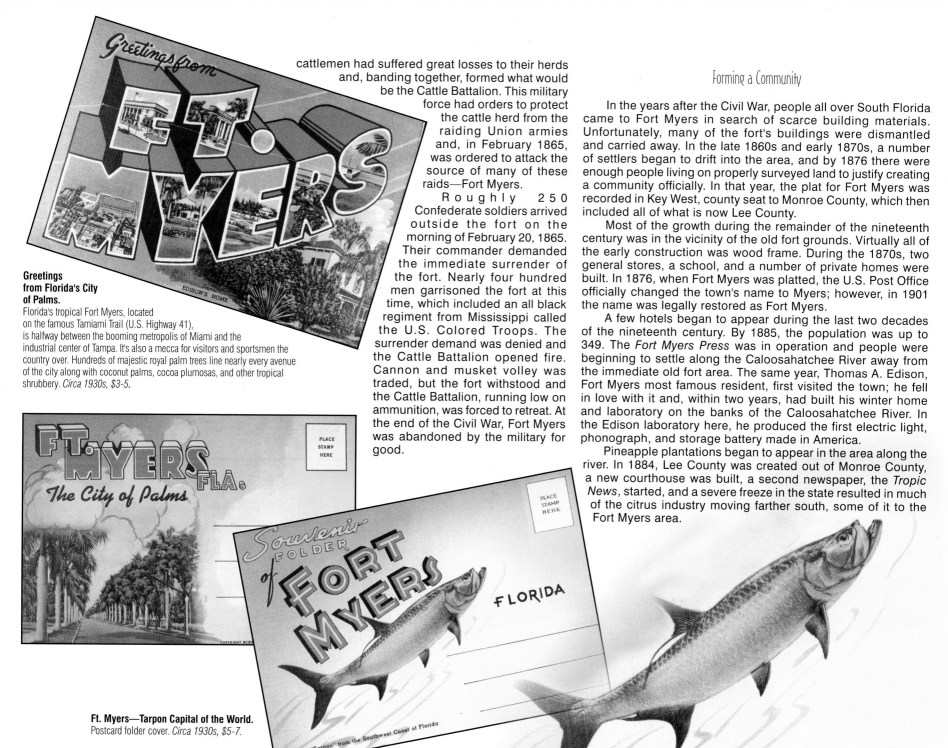

cattlemen had suffered great losses to their herds and, banding together, formed what would be the Cattle Battalion. This military force had orders to protect the cattle herd from the raiding Union armies and, in February 1865, was ordered to attack the source of many of these raids—Fort Myers.

Roughly 250 Confederate soldiers arrived outside the fort on the morning of February 20, 1865. Their commander demanded the immediate surrender of the fort. Nearly four hundred men garrisoned the fort at this time, which included an all black regiment from Mississippi called the U.S. Colored Troops. The surrender demand was denied and the Cattle Battalion opened fire. Cannon and musket volley was traded, but the fort withstood and the Cattle Battalion, running low on ammunition, was forced to retreat. At the end of the Civil War, Fort Myers was abandoned by the military for good.

Forming a Community

In the years after the Civil War, people all over South Florida came to Fort Myers in search of scarce building materials. Unfortunately, many of the fort's buildings were dismantled and carried away. In the late 1860s and early 1870s, a number of settlers began to drift into the area, and by 1876 there were enough people living on properly surveyed land to justify creating a community officially. In that year, the plat for Fort Myers was recorded in Key West, county seat to Monroe County, which then included all of what is now Lee County.

Most of the growth during the remainder of the nineteenth century was in the vicinity of the old fort grounds. Virtually all of the early construction was wood frame. During the 1870s, two general stores, a school, and a number of private homes were built. In 1876, when Fort Myers was platted, the U.S. Post Office officially changed the town's name to Myers; however, in 1901 the name was legally restored as Fort Myers.

A few hotels began to appear during the last two decades of the nineteenth century. By 1885, the population was up to 349. The *Fort Myers Press* was in operation and people were beginning to settle along the Caloosahatchee River away from the immediate old fort area. The same year, Thomas A. Edison, Fort Myers most famous resident, first visited the town; he fell in love with it and, within two years, had built his winter home and laboratory on the banks of the Caloosahatchee River. In the Edison laboratory here, he produced the first electric light, phonograph, and storage battery made in America.

Pineapple plantations began to appear in the area along the river. In 1884, Lee County was created out of Monroe County, a new courthouse was built, a second newspaper, the *Tropic News*, started, and a severe freeze in the state resulted in much of the citrus industry moving farther south, some of it to the Fort Myers area.

Greetings from Florida's City of Palms.
Florida's tropical Fort Myers, located on the famous Tamiami Trail (U.S. Highway 41), is halfway between the booming metropolis of Miami and the industrial center of Tampa. It's also a mecca for visitors and sportsmen the country over. Hundreds of majestic royal palm trees line nearly every avenue of the city along with coconut palms, cocoa plumosas, and other tropical shrubbery. *Circa 1930s, $3-5.*

Ft. Myers—Tarpon Capital of the World.
Postcard folder cover. *Circa 1930s, $5-7.*

Early 20th Century Developments

The twentieth century started with 943 residents in Fort Myers. The town experienced a building boom, resulting in a number of elaborately framed vernacular homes appearing along First Street and Palm Beach Boulevard.

The growth of the community was greatly facilitated in 1904 with the arrival of the Coast Railroad, which had its terminus at a dock on Monroe Street. In that same year, construction began on the Bradford Hotel, which still stands on Monroe Street. Several banks, a power plant, commercial ice plants, new hotels, and residential housing developments were part of the growth during the first two decades of the century. Streets in downtown Fort Myers were paved and the famous royal palms were planted along McGregor Boulevard.

The 1920s brought what was called the "Boom Time" to all of Florida, and Fort Myers shared in the riches. Most of the Mediterranean Revival buildings seen throughout the city were built during this period including commercial buildings in the downtown area and many private homes in all parts of Fort Myers.

In 1920, there were 3,678 people in Fort Myers. On April 15, 1925, there were 9,698, an increase of about three hundred percent in four years. The record of building permits issued tells a wonderful story. In 1920, there were approximately fifty issued; in 1924, 263—an increase in four years of better than eight hundred percent or an average of two hundred percent annually. In the first fourteen weeks of 1925, there were 519 issued. In 1920, there were but 5.5 miles of hard-surfaced roads in Lee County. In 1924, there were 64.4 miles and by January 1, 1926, there were over one hundred miles.

The 1920s also saw growth radiating out in all directions from downtown Fort Myers. Riverside Park, Edison Park, Seminole Park, Valencia Terrace, Alabama Groves, Allen Park, and other developments had their beginnings in the Boom Time. It was also during this time that the Seaboard Railroad came to town offering competition to Henry Plant's older coast line. Today three terminals from this period can still be seen in the city. The opening of the Tamiami Trail linked Fort Myers with Tampa and Miami and added even more to the fantastic growth during this time.

Trailer Camp.
Many visitors in the 1930s came to Florida by car with trailer in tow. Fort Myers had several trailer courts to accommodate these travelers. *Circa 1930s, $1-3.*

Citrus trees, forty years of age, and the magnificent royal palm trees furnish proof of the mildness of the climate. Fishing is one of the leading attractions. The fresh, brackish, and salt waters teem with such edible fish a pompano, Spanish mackerel, snappers, red and blue fish, sea trout and bass, revalia, and kingfish. A tarpon taken in the Caloosahatchee River by Peter P. Schutt measured 7'4" in length, 3'7" in girth, and weighed 208 pounds. Sportsmen find deer, bear, wildcats, wild turkeys, quail, and wild ducks.

Fort Myers is the winter homeport of many yachts and houseboats. A nine-foot channel from the Gulf of Mexico into the harbor is provided, as is a suitable wharf. Navigation companies operate boats regularly from Fort Myers to all river points and coast and inland resorts, where surf bathing is enjoyed every day of the year.

The Fort Myers golf course, two miles southwest on McGregor Boulevard, has eighteen links aggregating 6,388 yards in length, bogy 83, and par 74. McGregor Boulevard parallels the Caloosahatchee River to Punta Rassa on the Gulf, which is famed for its fishing and bathing. In the other direction, steamboats take passengers by the Caloosahatchee, Lake Okeechobee, and the Everglades Canal to West Palm Beach on the Atlantic Ocean.

Us Tin-Canners, Florida.

"Where the Iceman, cuts no ice —
Or the Gas, or the Coal, or the Rent-man, either"

Tin-Can Tourists.
"They drive tin cans and they eat outa tin cans and they leave a trail of tin cans behind them. They're tin-can tourists." So joked Floridians in the early decades of the twentieth century when they spotted the new breed of middle-class travelers who came south each winter to find a temporary place in the sun. Their cars were loaded down with stoves, blankets, tents, and as much housekeeping paraphernalia as could be strapped to the roof and running boards. Tin-Can Tourist Camps sprung up all over Florida after World War I when automobiles became inexpensive and popular. This type of tourist was not too welcomed, however, for they frequently pitched a tent and did their own cooking, thereby angering many of the hotel and restaurant owners in town. This postcard was mailed in Fort Myers. *Cancelled 1924, $8-10.*

Advertising Card. *Cancelled 1923, $1-3.*
This postcard was published by the Fort Myers Realtors Association and contained the following message:

From the heart of the tropics,
With its lure of eternal spring,
With a verdure that never
    defoliates,
With a riot of flowers in perennial
    bloom,
We bid you greeting, and with that
    greeting
We extend the warmth of a cordial
    and friendly invitation,
Come to Fort Myers.

Fort Myers Booklet.
This 24-page booklet, prepared by the Fort Myers Chamber of Commerce, presented a pictorial and descriptive picture of Fort Myers: The City of Palms. *Circa 1925, $25-30.*

ROYAL PALM, FORT MYERS, FLA.

Camping.
Camping under a canopy of Florida oak and palm trees was an unspoiled pleasure on the banks of the Caloosahatchee River in years gone by. *Circa 1910s, $5-7.*

Fort Myers Pennant.
Fort Myers is four hundred miles further
south than San Diego, California, and yet no farther
east than Cleveland, Ohio, snuggling next to the edge of
the Caloosahatchee River's rippling waters; a short ride from the
opalescence of the Gulf of Mexico. *Circa 1950s, $6-8.*

Florida Map Highlighting Fort Myers.
Circa 1925, $18-20.

Early Baseball

Baseball, the most American of all sports, came naturally to Fort Myers: the congenial place where big-leaguers play when their home grounds are snowed under, and the place where Thomas Edison, at age 80, knocked Ty Cobb off the pitcher's mound with a hard line drive.

The first recorded baseball game in Fort Myers was part of the young town's Independence Day celebration in 1896.

Fort Myers has been home to three of the four teams that played in the first two World Series games. The first end-of-season game between National League and American League victors took place in 1903. The Boston Red Sox won that series five to three against the Pittsburg Pirates.

Baseball hit big time in 1925 when the Philadelphia Athletics came to town. Before arriving here, they had won several pennants and three World Series games. In 1924, the city, anxious to have Fort Myers on the national sports map, built a baseball field complete with a wooden grandstand at the Lee County Fairgrounds, now called Terry Park. The Athletics spent a dozen prosperous seasons in Fort Myers. High-profile events included the guest appearance of Babe Ruth in the Athletics' uniform in March 1925, and two World Series wins, over Chicago in 1929 and St. Louis in 1930.

The Depression Years

Fort Myers suffered along with the rest of the state when a combination of poor publicity, hurricanes, and inadequate planning brought a collapse to Florida's Boom Time. The onset of the depression brought development and growth to a standstill all over the country. Still, there was moderate progress: some of the more elegant buildings in Fort Myers were built during this period including the Federal Building.

The mile-long Edison Bridge was also constructed during those years, making travel to the north much more convenient. It was dedicated—with the famous inventor present—in 1931. In a 'Believe It or Not' cartoon in 1935, Robert Ripley pointed out that the Edison Bridge was not illuminated, a condition remedied in 1937.

Construction of the Yacht Basin began in 1936; during World War II the U.S. Coast Guard was stationed here. After the war, the Yacht Basin became a municipal marina with a capacity of fifty boats. In 1972, the basin was expanded to handle 246 boats.

Fort Myers became the western terminus of the Cross-State Canal, connecting Florida's East and West coasts by way of the St. Lucie Canal, Lake Okeechobee, and the Caloosahatchee River.

World War II and Later

The big story in Fort Myers in the 1940s—as everywhere else in the world—was World War II. Throughout the state there were air bases to take advantage of Florida's fine flying weather. Lee County's air bases brought servicemen, and sometimes their families, to Fort Myers. Many of these people came back in later years to become permanent residents.

After World War II, Fort Myers grew, as did Lee County and the rest of Southwest Florida. Gradually vacant commercial and residential sites were filled in east along the Caloosahatchee River and south along Cleveland Avenue. New commercial buildings and shopping centers were built in all parts of the city. Fortunately, the older downtown area and much of the city's historic districts have retained much of their old charm.

Today, downtown Fort Myers is filled with antique stores, professional offices, restaurants, boutiques, jewelry stores, apartments, financial houses, and a convention center.

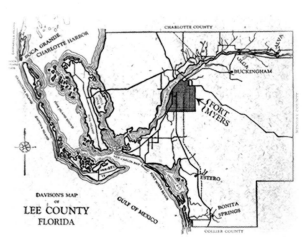

City Views

Below: Lee County Courthouse.
The handsome Lee County Courthouse at Fort Myers was completed in December 1915 at a cost of $100,000. In 1990, after seventy-five years of use, the structure was restored to its original state. It remains a vital part of the judicial complex, although a Justice Center has been constructed to serve a growing population. In the median between First and Bay streets stands a handsome monument featuring a bust of General Robert E. Lee, for whom the county was named. It was erected in 1966. The monument was unveiled a little more than one hundred years after the end of the Civil War. *Circa 1930s, $4-6.*

Court House, Fort Myers, Florida

LEE COUNTY COURT HOUSE, FORT MYERS, FLORIDA—44

Airplane View of Downtown Fort Myers.
This view shows the business section of Fort Myers; the Caloosahatchee River is on the left. *Cancelled 1929, $3-5.*

Courthouse Square.
Banyan tree on the Courthouse Square in Fort Myers, one of the better specimens in all of Florida, not only for its size, but for its formation as well. *Circa 1930s, $1-3.*

Unusual Banyan Tree, Court House Square, Fort Myers, Florida

Edison Plaque in City Park.
The citizens of Fort Myers erected this plaque in commemoration of Thomas Edison's 83rd birthday. *Circa 1930s, $3-5.*

The Iron Horse Arrives in Fort Myers.
In 1904, the Atlantic Coastline Railroad (ACL) arrived in Fort Myers. The Spanish-styled railroad depot (shown) opened in 1924 on Peck Street at a cost of $48,000. The structure, with its red barrel tile roof and parapets, included separate waiting rooms with large fireplaces and benches to provide ample seating for passengers. The complex had a ticket office, four restrooms, a telegraph office, and baggage rooms on the second story. The depot played a significant role in the economic development and population growth of the city. The ACL depot was used until 1971. It then stood vacant for a decade before being renovated and used in 1982 as the Fort Myers Historical Museum (now the Southwest Florida Museum of History). *Cancelled 1925, $16-18.*

A. C. L. RAILROAD STATION, FORT MYERS, FLORIDA.

Open Air Post Office, Fort Myers, Florida. City of Palms

Royal Palms and Open Air Post Office, Ft. Myers, Fla., "The City of Palms"

A Beautiful Home, Fort Myers, Florida.

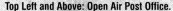

Top Left and Above: Open Air Post Office.
The Post Office, located on West First Street, opened October 30, 1933. It was a two-story reinforced concrete building of modified Spanish style. Across the front runs an open loggia with eight massive stone columns; at each end are enclosed lobbies finished in polychrome. Mangrove seeds occasionally sprout from fissures in the porous limestone of columns and facings. In 1965, the post office moved to its present site and the structure [shown later] became the Federal Building. Today, it is the Sidney and Berne Davis Art Center, a cultural and architectural centerpiece of downtown Fort Myers. *Circa 1930s, $3-5.*

Fort Myers Residences.
As more Northerners relocated to Fort Myers, more stately residences were built—of which many were used as scenery on Fort Myers postcards. *Circa 1920s, $1-3.*

Railroad through Palm Forest, Florida.

Lee Memorial Hospital.
The Robert E. Lee Hospital, located at Victoria and Grand Avenues, opened in 1916. In 1943 a new Lee Memorial Hospital opened on Cleveland Avenue. Since then, it has undergone numerous expansions. *Circa 1950s, $1-3.*

Above and Right: Railroad Reaches Bonita Springs and Naples.
As boom fever spread in Florida, the Atlantic Coast Line Railroad's presence in Florida grew. In 1924, the ACL served Fort Myers, but area business leaders wanted service extended south of the City of Palms to Bonita Springs, Naples, and Marco Island. The Fort Myers Southern Railroad was opened to Bonita Springs in 1925. A year later the railroad reached Naples. *Circa 1920s, $3-5.*

MIDWINTER SCENE, TRAVELING THROUGH AN ORANGE GROVE, FLORIDA.

Civic Center.
The Civic Center, built in 1943, faces the Caloosahatchee River on Edwards Drive at Hendry Street. The center welcomed military personnel stationed in Fort Myers at Page Field and Buckingham Army Air Field during World War II. After the war, the building served as the Lee County Chamber of Commerce. The structure was demolished in 2007. *Circa 1940s, $3-5.*

Exhibition Hall, Ft. Myers, Florida 135

Exhibition Hall.
The $200,000 Exhibition Hall in Fort Myers seated 1,000 people; it was seventy-eight feet wide and 127 feet long, with 9,906 square feet of floor space. Built in 1955, the hall played an important role in Fort Myers' cultural and social life before it was demolished in 2007. Many entertainers appeared there, including comedian Milton Berle and singer Elvis Presley. *Circa 1955, $3-5.*

Residence of Clarence Chadwick.
Clarence Bennett Chadwick, inventor of forgery-proof paper for bank checks, built this home on First Street in 1925. The house featured twelve-inch thick concrete walls. Set off by beautiful palm trees, the house commands the attention of everyone entering the city. Later occupied by the J. E. Hubinger family, it's now a law firm. *Cancelled 1931, $1-3.*

Left: Cracker House.

The term "cracker" refers to Florida's early cattlemen. During cattle drives, cattlemen would use the cracking sound of their whips to keep the cattle moving. The one-room Cracker houses were built from pine lumber. Porches were added as time went on, and kitchens were commonly added to the back side of the house. The exterior of the cracker houses were usually done in vertical "board and batten." Tin roofs reflected the heat of the sun rather than absorbing it. Doors and windows, positioned directly across from each other, helped create a breeze inside the house. The house shown — a replica located at the Southwest Florida Museum of History — is 12'x20'; the only pieces of furniture were a bed, table and chairs, trunk or dresser, and pie safe. *Author photograph.*

Murphy-Burroughs Home.

John T. Murphy, a millionaire cattleman and businessman from Montana, built a beautiful home on First Street that the local newspaper declared was one of the handsomest south of Tampa. With twenty-one rooms, it was the largest residence in Fort Myers in 1901. It was built of Florida pine and had indoor plumbing, electricity, seven fireplaces, a music room, beveled glass front door, a 15' x 17' library, an 11' x 16' reception hall, and a veranda that encircled the house. Murphy died in 1914; in 1919 the house was sold to businessman Nelson Thomas Burroughs. In the early years, the Burroughs home was the setting for many Fort Myers social gatherings. In 1983, the home was bequested to the City of Fort Myers. It has been restored and is once again a hub of social activity and a jewel in Fort Myers' crown of historic homes. *Cancelled 1923, $1-3.*

Field of Gladiolus.

Fort Myers visitors enjoyed driving on McGregor Boulevard, a highway lined with gigantic royal palms, which led to Lee County's vast flowering fields of gladiolus. The gladiolus crop earned Fort Myers the title of World Winter Glad Capitol. After the gladioli were harvested, sized, and boxed, they were shipped all over the country. Today, the gladiolus industry has disappeared. *Circa 1930s, $1-3.*

Southwest Florida Museum of History.

The Southwest Florida Museum of History arranges Fort Myers history into neat segments that take you back to the days of prehistoric mammals and ancient civilizations up through the eras of the Calusa Indians, Spanish exploration, fish camps, cattle driving, gladiolus farming, and World War II training. Outdoors there is a replica of a local early-1900s Cracker house, and the 84-foot-long *Esperanza*, a private Pullman railroad car that shows the luxury that was available to well-heeled rail travelers in the 1930s. *Author photograph.*

Municipal Yacht Basin.

The waterfront is an important part of life in Fort Myers. The City Yacht Basin bustles with boating activity, both private and commercial. Yachts crossing the state often stop at the marina here before heading to the East Coast or north along the Gulf of Mexico. The Yacht Basin was built during the Great Depression by the Work Projects Administration (WPA) at a cost of $300,000; the Basin was lined with coconut palm trees. *Circa 1940s, $1-3.*

Top: Esperanza.
The *Esperanza* is a traveling vehicle of luxury; the longest and one of the last private Pullman rail cars. While George Pullman's personal car measured sixty-seven feet, the *Esperanza* is eighty-four feet long and eleven feet wide. She is 101 tons of steel on wheels, a total of 202,900 pounds. She has a ten-foot lounge and four staterooms ranging from 6'4" to the master suite at 8'6". *Author photograph.*

Esperanza Lounge.
The walls are Cuban mahogany. Over the window to the left of the door are three gauges: a speedometer, clock, and a brake pressure gauge. Under the desk are hook-ups for a radio installed by the railroad when the *Esperanza* was used as an "office car." Outside the rear platform there are lights for night boarding and an adjustable mirror for viewing conditions along the train during switching. *Author photograph.*

Esperanza Dining Room.
The dining room is the largest room at 13'6", complete with built-in, floor to ceiling sideboard, and a table and chairs that can seat eight people comfortably, or expand for buffet service. To serve the dining room there is a 6'4-inch kitchen, a 3'2-inch pantry, and a porter's room. *Author photograph.*

Right: Aunt Jemima Steamboat.
The *Aunt Jemima* steamboat was designed and built by Albert Hansen for use around the Hansen Boatway. The *Jemima* was so named because it looked like a box of that pancake mix floating around on the water. The *Jemima* was easily turned and could run in very shallow water, making it perfect for pulling stored boats out of the covered boathouses at the boatyard. Another steamboat in Fort Myers was the *Gladys*, acquired by the Kinzie Brothers around the turn of the twentieth century. Like other steamboats of the era, the *Gladys* carried freight, passengers, and mail. Her regular route included stops at Fort Myers, Sanibel Island, Captiva Island, Useppa Island, and the communities of St. James City, Pineland, and Bokeelia on Pine Island. Steamboats were used extensively in Southwest Florida waters from the early 1900s to the 1930s, when improved and extended rail and road transportation resulted in a demise to the steamboat era. The *Aunt Jemima* is stored at the Southwest Florida Museum of History. *Author photograph.*

Right: Fort Myers' First Fire Truck.
By 1914, the citrus industry was an important business and Fort Myers was the site of the largest citrus packing plant in the world. The packing plant and much of the associated dock was destroyed by fire early in the year. As a result, the city of Fort Myers bought its first modern fire truck, an American LaFrance engine that cost $10,000. It is on display at the Southwest Florida Museum of History. *Author photograph.*

Left: Fort Myers Historical Museum.
After the Atlantic Coast Line Railroad discontinued service in 1971, the depot was saved from demolition when a group of concerned citizens felt it should be renovated. In April 1982, the depot opened as the Fort Myers Historical Museum and was later changed to the Southwest Florida Museum of History. The ACL depot, built in 1924, housed individual black and white waiting rooms, ticket windows, and bathrooms cordoned off by a brass railing due to segregation at that time. Both waiting rooms featured beautiful fireplaces. When built, the depot had no air conditioning. Museum brochure. *Circa 1982, $1-3.*

Right: Ireland's Dock.
Shortly after 1900, the dock, located at the foot of Hendry Street, was used by George F. Ireland as an oil and fuel distribution center, and became known as Ireland's Dock. It was later used as a service wharf for houseboats and yachts. The Fort Myers Yacht Basin was later built here. *Circa 1910s, $3-5.*

A 15855 On the Caloosahatchee, Fla.

On the Caloosahatchee.
The Caloosahatchee River, shown as it was in the early days, sometimes winding between white, sandy beaches or high, rocky banks, sometimes through dense tropical growth or beside stretches of open grass lands. *Cancelled 1910, $6-8.*

A THATCHED HOUSE ON THE BANKS OF THE UPPER CALOOSAHATCHEE RIVER, FLA.

Family Scene Along the River.
The 75-mile long, black water Caloosahatchee River begins in Lake Okeechobee, the second largest freshwater lake entirely within one state, and ends in the Gulf of Mexico near Punta Rassa. The Caloosahatchee is part of the Okeechobee Waterway, Florida's only cross-state waterway. *Cancelled 1916, $8-10.*

THE CALOOSAHATCHEE RIVER ABOVE FORT MYERS, FLA.

Caloosahatchee River.
This picturesque river flows from its source in Lake Okeechobee to the west, providing in such a vast expanse of water, with a width at Fort Myers of close to three miles, an efficient drain for all of Lee County's watershed. The river empties into San Carlos Bay, which is protected from the Gulf of Mexico by Sanibel Island. *Circa 1920s, $1-3.*

Chapter Two:
Traveling by Water & Land

Along the Caloosahatchee River

Looking Northwest from Downtown Fort Myers.
Fort Myers was the first large city on the Caloosahatchee River. The river's name translates to "river of the Caloosa (Calusa)," and the river serves as the westernmost link of a cross Florida waterway. The banks of the Caloosahatchee range the full gamut from very heavy, high-rise type development to all-natural stretches. *Circa 1990s, $1-3.*

CALOOSAHATCHEE RIVER FRONT, FORT MYERS, FLA.

Caloosahatchee Riverfront.
A busy morning on the Caloosahatchee riverfront, which stretches for several miles along the southern shore of the river. In the early 1900s, as Fort Myers was gradually becoming a winter resort for the wealthy and famous of the day, the Caloosahatchee riverfront grew congested. During the season, private yachts, skiffs, and steamboats maneuvered for dock space. This view shows some of the boat designs of the period. *Circa 1910s, $4-6.*

Fishing on the Caloosahatchee River, Fort Myers, Florida.   41

Fishing on the Caloosahatchee River.
The waters of Caloosahatchee River and the Gulf of Mexico abound with sport and game fish of many varieties. The silver king tarpon makes its home in Fort Myers waters. The angler can cast in any direction, off any pier, or troll through the waters of this mystic paradise and come home smiling and content. *Circa 1930s, $3-5.*

Above: Shrimp Fleet.
Shrimp trawlers docked along the palm-lined Caloosahatchee River. Catching and processing shrimp was an important industry in Fort Myers. *Circa 1930s, $3-5.*

Below: A Shrimp Catch.
A view at the Shrimp Fleet Headquarters on the Caloosahatchee River. *Cancelled 1957, $3-5.*

Right: Thomas A. Edison Memorial Bridge.
The Thomas A. Edison Memorial Bridge opened in 1930, however, the opening ceremony was delayed until February 11, 1931 in honor of Edison's 84th birthday. This bridge, which spans the Caloosahatchee River, is the first sight tourists see of Fort Myers as they drive south from the north. Prior to this, the only bridge crossing the river had been the wooden Fremont Bridge in East Fort Myers, which was built in 1924 and burned in the early 1940s. *Circa 1930s, $3-5.*

Overlooking the Caloosahatchee River.
Mr. and Mrs. Thomas A. Edison enjoyed a lovely view of the Caloosahatchee River from the veranda of Seminole Lodge, their winter home in Fort Myers. *Circa 1990s, $1-3.*

The Bridge at Alva.
Development of the motor car brought pressure for improvements to highways, but roads and bridges were costly and the funds to build them were scarce. This steel-framed bridge was built across the Caloosahatchee River at Alva, east of Fort Myers. *Circa 1920s, $1-3.*

A View of the River from the Edison Estate.
The Caloosahatchee River winds down from Florida's northern Everglades into the sunlit Gulf of Mexico. On its banks are bright orange groves, and alligators doze lazily on its mud flats. As it drifts by the palm-lined city of Fort Myers, it passes one spot lovelier than any other—the home, gardens, and laboratories where inventor Thomas Edison lived and worked for nearly half a century. The abundant bamboo growing wild along the river was one of the factors that enticed Edison to make Fort Myers his winter home. He used Japanese bamboo as a filament in his electric lamps for almost a decade. Today there are eight varieties of bamboo growing in the gardens. Shown are Edison's Lily Pond and Pier on the river. *Circa 1930s, $2-4.*

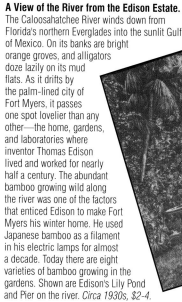

Tropical Lily Pool and Dock

Edison Memorial Bridge at Night, Fort Myers, Florida

Moonlight View of the Caloosahatchee.
Electric lights—an Edison invention— were added to the Edison Bridge in 1937. *Circa 1940s, $1-3.*

Cross-Florida Waterway.
Boats can travel across Florida by using the Caloosahatchee River, Lake Okeechobee, and the St. Lucie Canal; they connected Fort Myers with the East Coast cities of Stuart and Palm Beach. *Circa 1930s, $4-6.*

BOAT ENTERING LOCKS, LAKE OKEECHOBEE, FLA.

Changing Streets and Byways

First Street.
The post-Civil War era brought South Florida its first wave of settlers. In 1866, Manual A. Gonzalez and Joseph Vivas took up residence at recently abandoned Fort Myers. Arrival of other settlers led to the establishment in 1876 of a post office. First Street was delineated in 1901, with frame buildings housing stores and offices lining it. Banks, a theatre, a church, a school, and the Keystone Hotel, which first welcomed Thomas Edison in 1886, occupied locations along its route. Railroad construction and tourism, twin forces for growth in late nineteenth century Florida, contributed to community expansion. The paving of First Street to ease the way for tourists and automobiles and the construction of "modern" buildings reflected early twentieth century attitudes among many Floridians. Electrification of the city street lights in the early 1920s symbolized the onset of Florida's Boom Period, an era of rapid growth especially significant in South Florida history. By 1940, Fort Myers was slowly overcoming the disastrous effects of the Depression, and First Street was crowded with businesses and tourists. *Circa 1950s, $3-5.*

Looking East on First Street.
The Bradford Hotel is shown on the left and the neoclassic-style First National Bank, built in 1914, is on the right at the intersection of Hendry Street. The First National Bank was the city's first granite structure; it's now occupied by law offices. This intersection is also the historical heart of Fort Myers' business district. *Circa 1940s, $3-5.*

Main Thoroughfare, First Street, Business Section, Fort Myers, Fla.

F-53—First Street, Fort Myers, Fla.   "Florida Moonlight over Royal Palms"

Moonlight over the Royal Palms on First Street.
Corporal Archie Hamilton, who was stationed at the Fort Myers Gunnery Training School, sent the following message to his family in Viola, Arkansas: "I got Violet's letter yesterday and wrote you all a letter last night. Didn't get any mail today. I am on K.P. tomorrow so I will have to get up at 3 o'clock. It sure was hot down here today." *Cancelled 1943, $2-4.*

Stately Royal Palms, Florida 37

Beautiful First Street, Fort Myers, Florida

F-36 FIRST STREET, FORT MYERS, FLA.

Beautiful Palm Lined First Street.
Thomas A. Edison was responsible for the wholesale planting of royal palms in Fort Myers. In 1907, the Town Council approved a plan presented by Edison to take care of a large number of royal palms, which he imported from Cuba and planted at his own expense. Now there are over 10,000 royal palms, cocos plumosas, and coconut palms in the city. *Circa 1930s, $1-3.*

Royal Palms Along McGregor Blvd. near Thomas A. Edison Winter Home, Ft. Myers, Fla.

Entrance to Edison Park. MacGregor Boulevard, Fort Myers, Florida

Entrance to Edison Park.

The statue *Rachel at the Well*, at the entrance of the Edison Park subdivision, is located on McGregor Boulevard—across the street from Edison's home. It was sculpted in 1926 by Helmut von Zengen and was modeled after the statue at the entrance to Chestnut Hill, a suburb of Philadelphia. Edison's wife, Mina, speaking on the behalf of women who were offended by the statue's nudity, talked the developer, James Newton, into draping Rachel with a toga. *Circa 1930s, $1-3.*

McGregor Blvd., Beach Road, Fort Myers, Florida   FM-128

MacGregor Boulevard, Fort Myers, Florida

Palm-Lined McGregor Boulevard.

Once a military trail during the Second Seminole War (1835-1842), a cattle trail during the Civil War (1861-1865), and Riverside Drive in the early 1900s, in 1915 the road was named McGregor Boulevard. Affectionately nicknamed the "Boulevard of Palms," it is lined with approximately 1,800 royal palms. Running parallel the Caloosahatchee River from downtown Fort Myers to Punta Rassa, this palm-lined highway leads visitors from downtown Fort Myers to Lee County's vast flowering fields of gladiolus, the Fort Myers Beach playground, and the shell-strewn islands of Sanibel and Captiva. *Circa 1930s, $1-3.*

McGregor Boulevard

Royal Poinciana Tree amidst Majestic Royal Palms, First Street

Royal Poinciana Tree Amidst Majestic Royal Palms, First Street.
Circa 1940s, $1-3.

Chapter Three:

Where to Stay and What to Do

Hotels

The Four-Story Royal Palm Hotel.
The Royal Palm Hotel helped transform the cow town of Fort Myers into a famous winter resort. It boasted that it was the first building in town wired for electricity. Over the years, the Royal Palm doubled in size and played host to millionaires and celebrities. *Circa 1915, $6-8.*

Beach Hotel on Fort Myers Beach. *Circa 1940s, $3-5.*

Lakeside Court.
This court was located one mile north of Fort Myers on the Tamiami Trail (U.S. Highway 41). It consisted of two-room units arranged in a semi-circle around a man-made lake. *Circa 1930s, $3-5.*

Bradford Hotel.
The Bradford Hotel was one of the most historic buildings in Fort Myers. Built in 1905, it was the second brick building constructed in town. Named in honor of Bradford D. McGregor, the hotel had forty-one rooms and a large dining room on the second floor. The hotel later expanded to one hundred rooms and added a downstairs dining room. The hotel was popular with wealthy sportsmen who came to Fort Myers in the winter for hunting. The Bradford was located on First Street in Fort Myer's business district. The hotel was later converted into law offices and condominiums. *Circa 1950s, $6-8.*

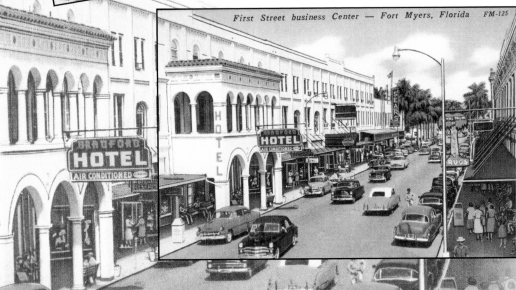

FRANKLIN ARMS HOTEL, FORT MYERS, FLORIDA

Franklin Arms Hotel.
The Franklin Arms contained over one hundred rooms and an attractive roof garden with pergola after the eight story annex was added in the late 1920s. During the Fort Myers boom, a human fly hustled up the tall hotel, pausing to stop at each floor to tell spectators what a buy they could find in Palmlee Park, a new subdivision. The Franklin Arms was the tallest structure in Fort Myers. *Circa 1930, $5-7.*

A Message from the Franklin Arms Hotel.
Emily mailed this card to Mrs. R. Daniel Frame in Reading, Pennsylvania and wrote, "We are going to have lunch here in a few minutes. We just saw Edison's, Edsel Ford's, and Firestone's homes. The palms here are lovely." *Cancelled 1935, $5-7.*

FRANKLIN ARMS HOTEL, FORT MYERS, FLORIDA

HOTEL ROYAL PALMS, FORT MYERS, FLORIDA

A Message from the Royal Palm Hotel.
The sender of this card from Fort Myers to Passaic, New Jersey wrote: "This is fine. Just like summer. A hard place to get to, but also hard to leave. I may have a swim before we leave." *Cancelled 1910, $6-8.*

Front Entrance to Royal Palm Hotel, Fort Myers, Fla.

Royal Palm Hotel.
The Royal Palm Hotel was one of the most prestigious hotels in Fort Myers for decades. Erected in 1898 by Hugh O'Neill at a cost of $70,000 and operated as the Fort Myers Hotel, it was purchased in 1905 by General M. O. Terry. The hotel got its name from the fact that in its heyday there were eighteen different varieties of palm trees planted on its grounds. The Royal Palm was demolished in 1948. *Cancelled 1912, $10-12.*

Hotel Royal Palm, Fort Myers, Florida.

Royal Palm Hotel.
Of constant interest to the winter visitor was the Cannon-ball tree in the Royal Palm Hotel grounds, the only tree of its kind in North America. It belongs to the same family as the Brazil nut and bears a round fruit that exactly resembles a rusty cannon ball. *Circa 1903, $6-8.*

Recreation

**Playing Golf
in the City of Palms.**
Fort Myers is obsessed with golf. Superb golf course communities encircle the city, which is home to four excellent public golf courses. There are other golf courses located in Bonita Springs and Naples, and the islands of Sanibel and Captiva. *Circa 1950s, $3-5.*

Cape Coral Gardens.
The Gardens (Rose Gardens) were one of Cape Coral's leading attractions. The Gardens, located northwest of Fort Myers, included a trained porpoise show, a synchronized colored lights water show, and gardens with exotic plants, animals, and strolling peacocks. The attraction closed in 1970. Shown: the friskiest, friendliest inhabitants of the sea perform amazing acrobatics in a show conducted from the stern deck of a "wrecked" Spanish galleon at Cape Coral Gardens. *Circa 1955, $4-6.*

Fish Tales.
Located outside the Thomas Edison Guest House sitting room, this tarpon serves as a memento of the Edisons' fishing adventures. In 1904, while fishing the Caloosahatchee River aboard the *Reliance*, fourteen-year-old Charles Edison caught this one hundred-pound tarpon, beating his father's forty-pound catch. Charles related later in life that it was the only time he beat his father at something, and it was remembered as a family joke for years. Fishing was a favorite hobby of the entire Edison family. In a 1906 letter Edison notes, "The finest tarpon fishing in the world is right in front of my house in Florida." *Circa 1990s, $1-3.*

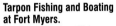

**Tarpon Fishing and Boating
at Fort Myers.**
Located on the beautiful Caloosahatchee River, the coconut palm-lined Fort Myers Yacht Basin is home to many boats. Boaters fishing around the waters of Fort Myers can expect to find grouper, Spanish mackerel, snook, shark, tripletail, red snapper, tarpon, barracuda, cobia, king mackerel, amberjack, and permit. The mouth of the Caloosahatchee River is dotted with oyster bars; these combined with swift currents provide great fishing. *Circa 1930s, $3-5.*

Churches

Methodist Church, Fort Myers, Fla.

O'Neill Memorial Methodist Church.
There are strong and progressive congregations in each of the seven denominations represented among Fort Myers churches. These congregations were always ready and anxious to make it pleasant for the transient visitor or to welcome among them those who came to stay. Shown is the O'Neill Memorial Methodist Church, located across from the Royal Palm Hotel on First Street at Royal Palm Avenue. Hugh O'Neill, who built the Royal Palm Hotel, donated the money for a new church in memory of his only son, Hugh O'Neill, Jr. The church, built in 1903, is surrounded by beautiful royal palm trees. *Circa 1920s, $1-3.*

First Baptist Church, Fort Myers, Fla.

First Baptist Church. *Circa 1940s, $1-3.*

Methodist Church — Fort Myers, Florida   FM-131

Methodist Church.
This Methodist Church, built in 1953, replaced an earlier church that was built in 1903. *Circa 1950s, $1-3.*

Dining Hall and Dinner Bell.
The dinner bell is all that is left of the three-story dining building, which was demolished in 1949. The first floor was the dining area for all members living in the Settlement. The second and third floors were dormitory rooms for sisters and young girls. The sleeping spaces were separated by cloth hung from ropes for privacy. Constructed in 1897 or 1898, the Dining Hall (which appears on page 39) was once the largest structure in Lee County. *Author photograph.*

Koreshan Unity Settlement

The Koreshan State Historic Site is located in Estero, just southeast of Fort Myers. The site contains nineteenth century structures and gardens remaining from a religious community that settled here. Koreshan was one of a number of utopian, communal societies that formed near the end of the nineteenth century.

The founding of the Koreshan Unity Settlement in Estero, Florida, was the continuation of a movement started in Moravia, New York, in 1880 by Dr. Cyrus R. Teed. His religious utopian community of two hundred followers often had to contend with an unfriendly and hostile society because of their religious, scientific, and cultural beliefs. In its efforts to establish and maintain an environment favorable to its development and growth, the movement relocated to the Florida frontier in 1894.

As the community's leader, Dr. Teed took the name "Koresh," the Hebrew translation for Cyrus, meaning shepherd. His colony, known as the Koreshan Unity, believed, among other things, that the entire universe existed within a giant, hollow sphere.

Encouraged by their visionary leader, the industrious Koreshans built and operated a printing facility, boat works, cement works, sawmill, bakery, store, and hostelry. Education, science, and art also helped shape their community. Education served an important role, not only for the children at the settlement but also for the adult members. Artistic endeavors included producing plays and musicals, and creating elaborate Victorian gardens. They also conducted scientific experiments related to their beliefs about the earth.

After the death of Dr. Teed in 1908 at the age of 69, membership of his religious group began to decline. In 1961, the four remaining members deeded 305 acres of their land to the State of Florida as a park and memorial. The Koreshan Unity Settlement Historic District is on the National Register of Historic Places.

Settlement Education

Education played an integral part in the Koreshan Unity. Dr. Teed believed a person should be prepared to lead a useful, productive, and happy life. Schooling was provided for all members of the Settlement. Children learned the three R's in the morning and vocational education in the afternoon. They had "jobs" in the Settlement's businesses. They were also encouraged to take music lessons and participate in the theatrics. For the adults, there were lectures on art, Koreshan cosmogony and doctrine, osteopathy and dentistry, history and ethnology, music and music composition, and "Higher Mathematics from the Koreshan standpoint." Other topics of more general nature were presented occasionally by visiting speakers. A library was planned, but never built. Literature was available to the members and included popular novels and poetry in addition to medical, religious, and philosophical works.

Far Left: Damkohler House. When Dr. Cyrus Teed arrived, this cottage was the only structure on the property. It was built by Gustave Damkohler, a German homesteader, in 1882. *Author photograph.*

Near Left: Founders House. The Founders House, built in 1896, is the oldest surviving building in the Settlement. Much of the original framework survives. *Author photograph.*

Planetary Court. The Planetary Court was the home for women of the Planetary Chamber, the governing council of the Koreshan Unity. Built in 1904, it is a two-story structure with four rooms on each floor. One room was an office where the Planetary Chamber met. A cupola on the roof was living space for Henry Silverfriend, who was protection for the women. *Author photograph.*

Dr. Cyrus R. Teed Standing Beside A Tarpon. *Circa 1902.*

Art Hall. The Art Hall, circa 1905, served as the center for cultural, social, educational, and religious activities. *Author photograph.*

Left Column:

Vesta Newcomb Cottage.
During the 1930s, this house was moved to its present location. It was used as a residence for Settlement members. *Author photograph.*

Members Cottage.
This simple unpainted cottage was moved to the Settlement in the 1930s. It is typical of the houses members occupied. *Author photograph.*

New Store.
The New Store was built in the 1920s to take advantage of traffic on the Tamiami Trail. The building served as a general store, restaurant, post office, and dormitory. The Old Store, circa 1902, was located on the Estero River. Traffic to the Old Store was mostly by boat. The building burned around 1926 after the New Store had been built. *Author photograph.*

Above and Right: Generator and Machine Shop Buildings.
The Generator Building housed the electrical alternator, generator, and power source for generating AC electricity for the Settlement. The Unity generated electricity from 1916 until Florida Power and Light arrived in 1946. *Author photographs.*

Top: The Dining Hall and Kitchen at the Settlement. *Circa 1910s.*

Bottom: Bakery.
Constructed in 1903, this was where bakers produced 500-600 loaves of bread per day. Surplus was sold in the Koreshan store. The ovens were located on a cement slab in front of the building. *Author photographs.*

Koreshan Boat—Blue Bird.
Circa 1910s.

Landscape and Gardens

The land was a wilderness in 1894. The gardens were laboriously carved out of thick mangroves, pine trees, scrub oaks, and saw palmettos. Dr. Teed corresponded with other horticulturists, exchanging seeds and plants, and he was instrumental in the development of the gardens.

The sandy soils of Florida were quite a contrast to the rich Illinois farmland previously cultivated by the pioneers. They learned from their neighbors and soon found success with a variety of vegetables, mainly tomatoes, cow peas, sweet potatoes, greens, and beans. Some vegetables were grown commercially and shipped, but the farming and gardening were the mainstays of the Koreshan tables.

Descriptions from various Koreshan publications describe two types of orchards: those consisting of a single type of fruit tree, such as orange or grapefruit, and orchards of a mixed variety of fruit trees, including avocado, lemon, lime, mango, tamarind, fig, olive, banana, guava, date, gooseberry, sugar apple, and coconut.

The Koreshans also developed gardens for purely aesthetic purposes, as a place for nourishing the spirit rather than the body. Exotic trees and plants, such as the Washingtonia Palms, the eucalyptus, and the bamboo, played significant roles in the garden plans of the community.

The gardens featured mounds, terraces, and Arborvitae hedges. Trellises, gazebos, benches, and various ornamental fountains and urns also dotted the settlement landscape.

Estero River.
The Koreshan Unity Settlement was located on the Estero River. A bamboo landing provided a formal entrance from the river. Passengers and freight arrived here. Koreshans held concerts at the landing until they built the Art Hall. *Author photograph.*

Burial Mounds.
There were four mounds consisting of soil built up about three feet from the ground and ten feet in diameter; period photographs of them show concentric circles of crushed shell and grass. *Author photograph.*

Koreshan Settlement Grounds

The Koreshan Settlement reminds one of a "small city." There were many shell paths or streets, vegetable gardens, Victorian gardens, fruit tree orchards, a landing on the Estero River, and the following structures (which are still standing): Founders House, Planetary Court, Art Hall, New Store, Bakery, Vesta Newcomb Cottage, Conrad Schlender Cottage, two Machine Shops, Electric Generator Building, pole containing Dinner Bell, foot bridges, Damkohler House. The following structures are no longer standing: Old Store, Storage Shed, Laundry Building, Publishing House, School, Sawmill, Machine/Woodworking Shop, Boat Works, Concrete Works, and family cottages.

Sunken Gardens and Bridges.
The landscaped Sunken Gardens contained many exotic non-native plants. Finely crafted foot bridges connecting the Settlement to the Sunken Gardens; they led to an area referred to as "Monkey Puzzle Island." The Rustic wooden and the white Victorian bridges were constructed in 1904-1905. Replica bridges exist today. *Author photographs.*

Chapter Four:

Famous Winter Residents

Thomas Edison House

Edison-Fort Myers Timeline

1885: The frontier town of Fort Myers is incorporated. • Thomas A. Edison arrives by boat from St. Augustine and purchases property on the Caloosahatchee River.

1886-87: Two homes and a laboratory are built.

1888-1900: The Edisons do not visit Seminole Lodge due to difficulties with remote travel, young children, and business commitments.

1901: The family returns, and for several years after, traveling by rail as far as Punta Gorda and then by steamboat to Fort Myers.

1904: Rail travel is available to Fort Myers.

1906: Guest House is remodeled.

1914: Edison invites Henry Ford to Fort Myers.

1916: Henry Ford purchases the adjacent property and home.

1928: The original laboratory building is dismantled and reconstructed in Michigan. The Little Office and Moonlight Garden are created. The Pool area is remodeled and the Edison Botanic Research Laboratory is constructed.

1931: Edison spends his last season at Seminole Lodge.

Statue of Thomas A. Edison.
Image of the Edison statue (beside the large banyan tree and near the Edison Botanic Research Laboratory). *Author photograph; postcard, circa 1930s, $1-3.*

Thomas A. Edison (1847-1931).
No single American has matched the creativity of Thomas Edison. The inventor registered 1,093 patents, including seventy-five in 1882 alone: 141 for batteries, 150 for the improvements of the telegraph, and 389 for electric power and light. Edison not only developed his own ideas, he also improved those of others, including the telephone of Alexander Graham Bell. A shrewd businessman, he perfected a workable light bulb and then a meter to charge customers for the electricity they used. His Edison General Electric Company, founded in 1890, employed more than 7,000 people. The press dubbed him "The Wizard," however, Edison never pretended that inventing was easy. "Genius is one percent inspiration and ninety-nine percent perspiration" is one of his best known sayings. The $40,000 he made from inventing the stock market ticker-tape machine in 1871 freed him to become a full-time inventor. This is a clip-art drawing.

Popular Edison Quotes

• "I would like to live about three hundred years. I think I have ideas enough to keep me busy that long."

• "I find out what the world needs. Then I go ahead and try to invent it."

• "A man's best friend is a good wife."

Right: Edison's Executive Ediphone.
The dictating phonograph, first put on the market as an improved wax cylinder model in 1888, was called the Edison Commercial Phonograph. In 1905, the name was changed to Edison Business Phonograph. From 1916-1948 it was known as the Ediphone. Circa 1960s, $1-3.

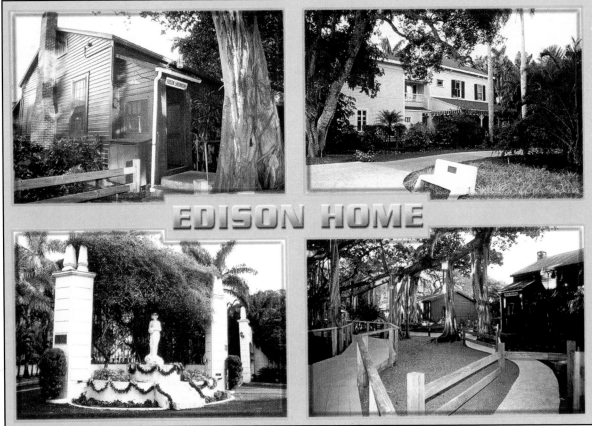

Above: Edison's Winter Home.
When Edison's widow, Mina, died in 1947, she willed
the house, laboratory, and thirteen acres of landscaping
exotica to the city of Fort Myers, which added a museum,
filling it with vivid evidence of the genius of this country's
most prolific inventor. Many of his patents are on display,
including dozens of Edison photographs, hundreds of light
bulbs, telephones, storage batteries, movie cameras, stock
ticker, and some of the automobiles presented to him by
neighbor and friend Henry Ford. *Circa 1948, $5-7.*

Left: Edison Home, Laboratory, and Gardens Brochure.
Circa 1940s, $5-7.

Thomas and Mina Edison.
The Edisons are shown in front of the laboratory where Thomas Edison conducted his last major experiment—the extraction of natural rubber from goldenrod. At right is an air-conditioned vault, the first in America, which Edison built for storing records. *Circa 1930s, $4-6.*

Edison in His Original Fort Myers Office.
Thomas Edison at his desk in his original laboratory office. Shown are a drafting table, desk, scales, and book shelves. *Circa 1920s, $3-5.*

Friendship Stones.
In 1928, Edison's wife Mina, started asking guests to send a stone to commemorate their visit. There is an unmarked stone that is understood to be from Henry Ford, noting, "He was just a poor farm boy." Over fifty stones create the Friendship Walk that starts near the gate at McGregor Boulevard and winds toward the Edison home. There is a similar walk at Rollins College in Winter Park. Dr. Hamilton Holt, president of the college, gave the first stone. Other stones are from friends, local dignitaries, and employees of Seminole Lodge. The Friendship Walk created a lovely entrance into the world of the Edisons. *Author photograph.*

F.2   WINTER HOME OF THE LATE THOMAS A. EDISON, FORT MYERS, FLA.

6A-H1436

A Great Man's Home.

Thomas Alva Edison found health and happiness in building a Queen Anne-style winter home and garden on the banks of the Caloosahatchee River in Fort Myers. Seminole Lodge, as his home was named, lies literally buried in a jungle of rare tropical shrubs, trees, and other plants, and is actually two houses connected by a breezeway; the family home section and the Edison Guest House. The Edisons and their visitors used the kitchen and dining room in the Guest House. Among guests at Seminole Lodge were Henry Ford, President Herbert Hoover, Harvey Firestone, and Charles Lindbergh. Designed by Edison, Seminole Lodge was built in sections in Fairfield, Maine in 1885. The sections were then transported to Fort Myers on four sailing schooners and erected in 1886. Circling the homes are large overhanging porches, which, combined with French doors on the first floor, provide a cool breeze through the home at all times. Electric chandeliers, "electroliers," were designed by Edison and hand made of brass in his own workshop. *Circa 1930s, $3-5.*

Thomas Edison's Home, Fort Myers, Florida 55

F.25—Thomas A. Edison Winter Home
Fort Myers, Fla.

Edison Botanic Research Laboratory.

The price of natural rubber rose dramatically during World War I and into the 1920s. Thomas Edison, Henry Ford, and Harvey Firestone combined their efforts, talents, and finances, and in 1927 they established the Edison Botanic Research Corporation. The laboratory (shown) was built in 1928 to replace the first Edison Fort Myers lab, which had been relocated to Henry Ford's collection of historic buildings in Greenfield Village, Michigan. Here, Edison tested a large variety of plants and finally focused on goldenrod, a common weed growing to an average height of three to four feet and which yielded five percent latex. Edison was able to grow the goldenrod to a height of twelve feet, yielding twelve percent latex. Rubber research and experimentation continued after Edison's death under the leadership of his brother-in-law, however, in 1936 the corporation was dissolved because rubber production was not a commercial success. Edison had hoped to give America a domestic source of rubber in case war shut off supplies from the Orient. With his work unfinished, Edison died in 1931—ten years before the Japanese attack on Pearl Harbor and the start of World War II.
Author photograph.

Above: Interior View of Edison's Laboratory.

Fort Myers was the headquarters for Edison's last major experiment—the extraction of natural rubber from goldenrod. His test tubes, machinery, and equipment are on display in the laboratory. Edison died with this task unfinished, but a well worn tire made of his goldenrod rubber remains as a "spare" for his favorite Model T Ford. Also in the laboratory are many models of his earlier inventions, including phonographs with huge horns, and a replica of the original incandescent lamp. Edison's workshop team included a machinist and a glassblower to make bottles, flasks, and test tubes on site.
Circa 1930s, $1-3.

Left: Edison's Laboratory Office.

Laboratory office, with cot where Edison took catnaps during long working hours.
Circa 1930s, $1-3.

THOMAS A. EDISON HOME, FORT MYERS, FLORIDA—9

Seminole Lodge.
The Edisons shared the estate with their friends. After arriving in Fort Myers from a trip that took many days, guests stayed for weeks or months. Activities included boating, fishing, reading, picnics, playing board games, and walks around the grounds. *Circa 1920s, $4-6.*

Master Bedroom of Seminole Lodge.
The charming bedroom reflects the influence of Mrs. Edison's taste. Thomas generally deferred to Mina in matters pertaining to the home and children. This bedroom is located on the second floor and is accessible by an exterior staircase built in 1910. *Circa 1940s, $1-3.*

Edison House Surrounded By Beautiful Plants.
The Edison home with its fourteen-foot overhangs, expansive French doors, and high ceilings was a master piece of practicality for life in Florida at the beginning of the twentieth century. The Edisons first decided to paint the home gray in 1910; however the roof color has always been red. *Circa 1940s, $3-5.*

The Unique World of Thomas A. Edison.
Today the Edison home is as he left it in 1931 with original furnishings, books, pictures, and beautiful chinaware. The furnishings and architecture are reminiscent of a bygone era, yet there are many innovations that we do not have in many modern homes. The inventive genius of Edison is evident throughout his house. The Edison family purchased many items for the home from Proctor & Company of New York City. Shown is the Living Room in Edison's home. *Circa 1940s, $1-3.*

The Edison Bedroom

Living Room

Drawing Room

Edison's Portland Cement Swimming Pool

Drawing Room.
The French doors open onto the fourteen-foot veranda encircling the home and welcomes cooling breezes from the Caloosahatchee River. *Circa 1940s, $1-3.*

Elegant Dining at the Edison Guest Home.
One of only three in the world, the Haviland China Company turkey platter was given to the Edisons by President Rutherford B. Hayes in 1878. Edison designed and manufactured "electrolier" lighting fixtures in the early 1880s to accommodate his newest invention. There are fifteen located throughout the two homes. This one provides light to the dining room. *Circa 1940s, $1-3.*

Swimming Pool.
In the early 1900s, Edison built one of Florida's first swimming pools with cement from his own Edison Portland Cement Company. The swimming pool was built for his children and his guests as Edison did not believe in exercise. The pool was braced with native bamboo rather than the usual steel rods. It was filled by an artesian well that was 1,100 feet deep. The well was also used to irrigate the botanical gardens. *Circa 1930s, $1-3.*

Dining Room

F.26—Beautiful Swimming Pool
Thomas A. Edison Winter Home
Fort Myers, Fla.

Near Right: Edison's Caretaker's House.
Part of the Edison Caretaker's House existed on the land when Edison purchased the property from Samuel Summerlin in 1885. The cracker-style house was used as a stopover for cattle drovers moving herds down the old Wire Road (now McGregor Boulevard). Samuel Summerlin was the youngest son of Jacob Summerlin, one of the largest cattle owners in the state. In the early 1860s, Summerlin had a crude road constructed from Fort Ogden to Punta Rassa. He built shipping pens and a dock where boats went off to Cuba with cracker cattle and returned with commodities as flour and sugar. In 1903, Edison made the first round of additions to enlarge the house, and a 1928 addition had an apartment above and car and tool storage below. *Author photograph.*

Moonlight Gardens and Edison's Little Office.
The Little Office and Moonlight Gardens were added to the Edison estate in 1929. Together they form the shape of the 1886 laboratory, which was originally situated at this location. Henry Ford transported the laboratory, sand and all, to his 260-acre Greenfield Village in Michigan. He had earlier moved Edison's lab at Menlo Park with a few tons of Jersey soil to the site. To replace the lab, Ford commissioned to have the Moonlight Garden and Edison's Little Office built. Both were favorite spots of the Edisons in their later years at Seminole Lodge. Ellen Biddle Shipman, one of the first female landscape architects, designed the Moonlight Garden and filled it with blue and white flowers and a small pool to reflect the moonlight. Many of the flowers in the Moonlight Garden today could be found there in 1929. Charles Edison, the elder son of Thomas and Mina, later renamed this garden as the Memory Garden in honor of his mother. *Author photograph. Postcards, circa 1940s, $1-3.*

Above: Edison Pier.
The pier was the first structure to be built after Edison acquired the property. It reached out approximately 1,500 feet and was used to bring building materials to the property from barges anchored in the Caloosahatchee River. Later outfitted with boathouses, benches, and a summerhouse, it became a favorite spot for fishing and visiting. An avid bird lover, Mina Edison put birdhouses at the end of the pier to protect them from marauding cats. *Author photograph.*

Edison's Favorite Car—Model T Ford.
Edison loved automobiles, and in 1907, Henry Ford presented him a gift of a prototype Model T Ford. For the next twenty years, Ford had his engineers add the latest updates to the car every twelve months. Edison refused to part with the original for a newer version. The old car still runs, on display at the Edison Home and Museum. *Circa 1940s, $1-3.*

Edison's Model "T" Ford, Given Him by Henry Ford

View of the Fountain and Gardens.
The fountain, installed in 1907, was a popular gathering place for Edison and his guests. This spot provided a pleasant view of the gardens looking west toward the river or east toward McGregor Boulevard. *Circa 1930s, $1-3.*

ON THE ESTATE OF THE LATE THOMAS A. EDISON, FORT MYERS, FLORIDA—2

F.28—Giant Travelers Palm with Edison's Wheel Chair
Thomas A. Edison Winter Home
Fort Myers, Fla.

Giant Traveler's Tree With Edison's Wheel Chair.
In the final years of his life, Edison's doctor suggested that he use a wheelchair. Henry Ford, his friend and neighbor, although still agile and energetic, also bought a wheelchair so they might continue their "walks." The Traveler's tree, native to Madagascar, with a palm-like trunk, can grow to a height of twenty to thirty feet. The large leaf captures rainwater and stores it in the hollow stalks. *Circa 1930s, $1-3.*

Edison's Tropical Botanical Gardens.
Thomas Edison's love of botanical research and Mina's love of gardens combined to create a lush tropical paradise of exotic plants. There is a long avenue of huge mango trees filled with brilliant orchids. A giant sterculia alata from Africa towers eighty-feet in the air, topping even the immense Moreton Bay Fig with its serpentine roots and the tree hibiscus from the West Indies. There are camphor trees, Borneo screw pines, African sausage trees, golden sausage trees, frangipani, Celon gooseberries, the mountain ebony from India with its pale lavender flowers, bromeliads, bougainvillea, bamboo, the night blooming cereus from Mexico, cinnamon bark and coffee berry trees, and the cajeput with its cork-like bark. Edison's garden was one of the most complete in America, containing more than 1,000 varieties of plants. *Author photograph. Postcard, circa 1930s, $1-3.*

F.24—Orchid Lane, Thomas A. Edison Winter Home
Fort Myers, Fla.

Kigelia Pinnata (Sausage Tree)

Left: Kigelia Pinnata (African Sausage Tree).
Reddish flowers open at night and are pollinated by bats in Africa. At the Edison home they are pollinated by hand. The seedpods (sausages) weigh five to fifteen pounds. While the fruit resembles a sausage, it is not edible; it's used as medicine by the African natives. They worship this tree for its medicinal powers. Edison used to tell his guests that it was one of his breakfast trees; another, with flowers resembling fried eggs, was near his house. *Circa 1940s, $1-3.*

Below: Banyan Tree.
This banyan tree is located beside the Edison Laboratory. It was given to Edison by Harry Firestone in 1925. It was brought over from India growing in a butter tub and was two inches in diameter and four feet tall. This amazing tree now occupies an acre, and is understood to be the third largest in the world. This type of tree produced a white milky sap (latex) that could be used to create rubber. *Circa 1930s, $1-3.*

F-45   ROYAL PALM ROW IN FRONT OF THE LATE THOMAS A. EDISON ESTATE, FORT MYERS, FLA.

6A-H1586

Banyan Tree

Avenue of Palms.
Edison had the first 1.5 miles of royal palms brought from Cuba and planted along McGregor Boulevard—they now stretch for seven miles. The fence of Edison's property is on the right. On the left is the entrance to the Edison Park neighborhood. *Cancelled 1937, $1-3.*

Henry Ford House

Henry Ford Statue.

As a young man, Henry Ford worked as chief engineer at the Edison Illuminating Company in Detroit. He became an admirer when Thomas Edison not only listened but grew excited about Ford's dream of a gas-driven vehicle that would be practical and affordable. In 1898, Ford completed an improved version of a gas-powered vehicle he was working on. After two failed automobile companies, the Ford Motor Company was formed in 1903; while building cars, the company grew. Ford made nine different models between 1903 and 1908, when the Model T was introduced. Henry was on his way to fame and fortune as his automobile caught on with Americans. Customers loved the look and sturdy feel of the Model T and the $825 price tag. More than 10,000 Model Ts were sold in the first year. Over the next few years the price dropped to $290 and around fifteen million Model Ts had been built. In 1927, the Model T was replaced with the Model A. By 1931 over four million Model A's had been produced. On April 7, 1947, at the age of 83, Henry Ford died at his Michigan home. All over the world, people remembered the man who built the first affordable car for the masses. He was the man who put the world on wheels. This statue of Ford that is located at his winter home in Fort Myers. *Author photograph.*

Right Column: The Mangoes.

Henry Ford purchased this home in 1916, to spend his winters with his good friend and neighbor, Thomas Edison, and did so for fifteen years. Henry Firestone, the tire tycoon, also spent time with both men at the estates, intrigued by Edison's research in developing new sources of rubber. The winter estates of Ford and Edison played an important role in one of the most unique friendships in American history. The house had a large living room, dining room, butler's kitchen and pantry, and bathroom on the first floor. On the second floor were four large bedrooms, a large bathroom, a sleeping porch, trunk room, and closets. The Fords added two wings to the back of the house, providing a guest bedroom and quarters for a secretary and maid. *Circa 1990s, $1-3.*

Citrus Trees in Front of the Henry Ford Home.

The Henry Ford home fronted 177 feet on McGregor Boulevard and ran a depth of 480 feet to the Caloosahatchee River and included many citrus trees in addition to bamboo, guavas, mangoes, coconut, grapefruit, pomegranates, star fruit, gooseberry, and bananas. The grounds of both the Ford and Edison homes abound with nature's harvest of edible fruit. In fact, a tropical fruit inspired the naming of the Ford home, "The Mangoes." With the warm tropical climate serving as their incubator, exotic fruits ripen to the peak of perfection, filling the air with a tantalizing fragrance. Caretakers of the gardens would ship seasonal fruits north to the families and their friends throughout the year. Homemade jams and jellies were prepared and stored for the families to enjoy upon their return to Fort Myers. The house, built to withstand hurricanes, was unpretentious, roomy, and comfortable—a perfect get-away from the pressures of the burgeoning Detroit automotive industry. The Fords were private people and did little entertaining. Their favorite pastime was to hold a square dance in their living room. Ford would crank up the phonograph and often did the calls himself. *Circa 1920s, $5-7.*

Winter Home of Henry Ford.

Henry Ford, the motor king, preferred picturesque simplicity in his winter home in Fort Myers. Surrounded by a tropical garden of beautiful flowers and towering royal palm trees, the bungalow type home of Clara and Henry Ford is hailed as one of the beauty spots of Florida and is located within five blocks of the heart of the city. *Circa 1920s, $5-7.*

Near Left: China's Ambassador's Visit to Fort Myers.

Henry Ford and Thomas Edison, winter neighbors, entertained China's ambassador of goodwill, Tien Lai Huang; the three men are shown in front of Edison's laboratory. *Circa 1930, $5-7.*

The Mangoes
The Henry Ford Estate

F-23   WINTER HOME OF HENRY FORD, FORT MYERS, FLA.

HOME OF HENRY FORD, FORT MYERS, FLORIDA

Living Quarters.
The Fords often moved the lightweight wicker furniture to the porch so the living room could be used for square dancing. The fireplace in the living room was the only source of heat for the home. Adjacent to the living room, the Ford dining room is decorated in simple elegance. Clara and Henry Ford often watched tropical sunsets from their master suite veranda. This upstairs sun porch off the master bedroom, with its wicker furniture, overlooks the Caloosahatchee River. The second floor was off limits to everyone but the immediate Ford family with the second floor hallway leading to bedrooms, an office, and bath. Many famous friends enjoyed vacationing in the guest bedroom at the Ford home. *Circa 1990s, $1-3.*

Riverside Porch.
The Fords enjoyed warm Florida winters overlooking the Caloosahatchee River. In one view, a few of their vintage automobiles can be seen. *Circa 1990s, $1-3.*

Moreton Bay Fig Tree.
This Moreton Bay fig tree, with its monstrous configuration of roots, grows on the Ford property; it was imported from India. About half the roots of a fig tree are above ground. The tree is a cousin of the rubber tree. *Circa 1930s, $1-3.*

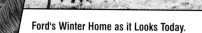

Ford's Winter Home as it Looks Today.
After Edison died in 1931, Ford stopped coming to Fort Myers. The visit of 1934 was the last time he stayed at the estate. Renting out the property for many years, Ford finally sold it in 1945 to local resident Thomas Biggar. In 1988, the Biggar property was sold to the City of Fort Myers. In September 1988, it was officially listed in the National Register of Historic Places. The Ford home was restored and opened to the public in 1990. *Author photograph.*

Part II: The Islands

Although the tribe of the powerful Calusa Indians is now extinct, ceremonial, burial, and refuse shell mounds are found on several islands including Mound Key, Pine, Sanibel, Estero, and Useppa. A look back at their history is provided here.

The Calusa Indians

Dating as far back as 2,500 years, the native Calusa Indians were the first-known residents of these islands. They lived along the Gulf Coast of the Florida peninsula from present day Sarasota southward to the Florida Keys. The Calusa Indians skillfully transformed the waterways around the island into abundant riches of food and tools. Oysters, clams, conchs, whelks, and other seafood were used for food, and their empty shells were crafted into tools. The Calusas proved to be skilled builders and craftsmen, perching their huts high atop shell mounds to provide protection from shore tides. Some of their shell mounds, which were also used for ceremonial burial and ritual sites, remain intact today.

Much of our information about the Calusa Indians comes from the son of a Spanish official stationed in Cartagena (present-day Columbia). The youngster, Hernando de Excalante Fontaneda, was shipwrecked along the Calusas' shores en route to Spain. He lived among the tribe for seventeen years, learned their language, and was the first white man to see the Everglades. In 1575, after returning to Spain, Fontaneda became the first man to write about Southern Florida and the Calusa people.

It is known that Juan Ponce de Leon, the man who claimed Florida for Spain, visited the Calusa Indians in 1513; Diego Miruelo made contact with them in 1516; and Hernandez de Cordova did in 1517. Ponce de Leon again landed among them in 1521, with the intention of establishing a settlement. But he offended his hosts, who attacked him and his men; Ponce de Leon was fatally wounded and the Spaniards were forced back to Cuba. When first discovered, the Calusa Indians were famous for the power of their chiefs, the amount of gold that they had obtained from Spanish treasure ships, and their addiction to human sacrifice.

Explorers who laid claim to Florida for Spain first wrote home about the Calusa Indians in 1513. During the time Spain ruled Florida, the Spaniards, always thorough record keepers, continued writing letters and reports about the Calusas. It was estimated that there were 3,000 Calusa Indians in 1650. An expedition sent into Calusa country in 1680 passed through five villages said to have a total population of 960.

Indians who lived in North Florida at the same time as the Calusas made their living by growing crops like corn, squash, and beans. The Calusa Indians did not farm; they made their living from the sea. Men and boys caught catfish, mullet, pigfish, and pinfish using nets made of palm fiber. From the shallow water around the islands, women, children, and the elders picked up shellfish such as oysters, clams, and conch. The Calusas also collected and ate fruits like seagrape and prickly pear as well as plant roots.

At the time when St. Augustine was settled attempts were made to establish a post among the Calusa Indians and to missionize them, but the post was soon withdrawn and the missionary attempt proved unsuccessful. The Calusas do not seem to have been converted to Christianity during the entire period of Spanish control.

Life by the sea affected the Calusas' towns as well as their diet. Most of their island homes were low-lying, just above sea level. Also hundreds of years of shellfish collecting by the Calusas and their ancestors meant that millions of discarded seashells lay all around their house and, after a while, people started building their houses on top of the shell heaps.

The Calusa Indian Society.
People lived and fished on Florida's Gulf coast long before the first pyramids in Egypt. Among the coastal dwellers from Sarasota to the Florida Keys were the Calusa Indians. What was the secret of their success? The estuary—an intricate system of sea grasses and mangrove trees and a magical mixing of fresh and salt water—provided food in such quantities that farming was never needed. The Calusas built towns, engineered canals, and developed a complex society. They eventually dominated South Florida. The Calusa legacy lives on, inspiring early pioneers and modern society to learn about and care for the coastal environment they called home. These blue-green waters still offer us food, recreation, and beauty. *Drawing by Merald Clark appears in the Calusa Indian exhibit at the Florida Museum of Natural History in Gainesville.*

Sanibel's Vanished People.
About 2,500 years ago the fierce Calusa Indians inhabited Sanibel and Captiva Islands, thriving on the island's bountiful natural resources. Throughout most of their existence, the Calusas lived off the land. Excavations on Sanibel have turned up flint and whelk projectile points, pots of clay, shell implements, and tools crafted from deer antlers. Varieties of shellfish were a major source of food as well as construction material. The Calusa Indians lived a simple existence; everything they needed was close at hand in the woodlands or sea. Shell mounds on Sanibel Island are a testament to a once flourishing culture. In the 1500s, the gold-hungry Spaniards discovered the island paradise. Sadly, the majority of the native islanders were wiped out and the few remaining either died in Cuban prison camps or fled into the Everglades with some of the early Seminole Indians. This village is on display at the Bailey-Matthews Shell Museum in Sanibel. *Author photograph.*

Later still, the Calusas shaped the shell heaps into flat-topped mounds and dug canals across the islands to make canoe travel easier and safer. Some of the shell mounds stood more than thirty-feet high. Today some islands are made almost entirely of the discarded shells of the Calusas and the people who came before them. Nine Indian mounds filled with pottery shards, fishhooks, and arrowheads have been found on Gasparilla Island.

Some of the shell mounds were the center of village life. The Calusa Indians gathered there for social occasions and ceremonial fetes while at the same time fleeing there for safety when storms lashed at the islands and waves swept across the low-lying land.

Because fishing was key to the Calusa Indians' survival, they created fishing gear using tools they had made from shark teeth. Also using seashell tools, they built large canoes of hollowed-out pine logs. These canoes were so well made they were capable of reaching Cuba. They sailed the open seas, sometimes with two canoes lashed together, propelled by paddles and sails woven of strips from palm fronds.

The Calusa Indians used pottery for drinking, eating, and cooking. Unlike other Indian tribes, the Calusas focused less on making pottery and more on using shells to create tools, jewelry, and utensils and many of their pottery shards have been found throughout Southwest Florida. The pottery that they made was plain, practical, and limited to a few simple shapes like bowls and jars.

The end came for the Calusa Indians, as well as other Indian tribes, in the 1700s. European diseases—such as measles, chicken pox, tuberculosis, yellow fever, and smallpox—took their toll on Indian peoples. Fighting enemies who had guns also killed many of the Calusas. By 1763, after years of poverty and hardship, the last few Calusa Indians set out for Cuba, leaving Florida forever. *(More information about the Calusa Indians appear in the chapters about Pine Island and Mound Key.)*

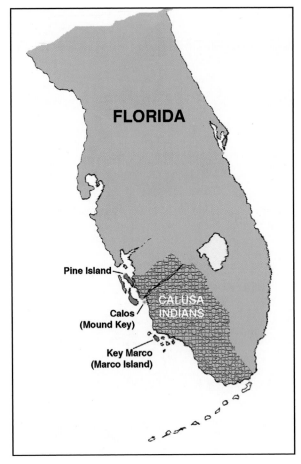

Calusa Influence in Southwest Florida.
Drawing shows the area of the Calusa Indians influence at the time of European contact in the sixteenth century.

Calusa Indian Carving A Mask.
History informs us that probably around 4000 B.C. the Calusa Indians or their ancestors inhabited Key Marco. These Native People had built large mounds using sand and millions of shells and fish bones that offered them protection from hurricanes. The mounds were also used for religious temples and burial sits. The Calusa Indians were crafty and intelligent woodworkers, who constructed canoes, beams, and planks for their houses, docks, and piers. Wood was the medium of Calusa expression. It played a role in every facet of life, from canoes to containers, tools to masks, and weaponry to ornaments. Excellence in woodworking is a hallmark of Calusa culture. Some of the Calusa Indians best known artifacts are carved masks and figureheads. *This drawing of a Calusa man carving a wooden mask with a shark-tooth tool was part of the Calusa Indian exhibit at the Florida Museum of Natural History in Gainesville, Florida. Drawing by Merald Clark.*

First Inhabitants.
Gasparilla Island's first inhabitants were the Calusa Indians, who lived there by A.D. 800 or 900. Charlotte Harbor was the center of the Calusa Empire, where thousands of people lived in fishing villages on the mainland and nearby Gulf islands. Nine Indian mounds—filled with pottery sherds, fish hooks, and arrowheads—have been found on Gasparilla Island, with more than two hundred additional sites located on nearby islands.

Chapter Five:
Sanibel Island

Sanibel Island, as well as nearby Captiva Island, features a history rich in intrigue and adventure, from the Calusa Indians, to Spanish explorers, infamous pirates, brave pioneers, and shell hunting tourists.

Historians believe that Sanibel and Captiva were formed as one island about 6,000 years ago from sediment that rose from the sea after being shaped by centuries of storm activity.

Spanish Explorers and Pirates

Famous explorer Juan Ponce de Leon is believed to have landed on Sanibel Island, naming it "Santa Isabella" after Spain's Queen Isabella, but the Spanish were unsuccessful in establishing any kind of permanent settlement.

Legend has it that the barrier islands soon became a haven for infamous pirates. "The Buccaneer Coast" attracted the notorious Jose Gaspar (Gasparilla) to the region in the early 1800s, where it was rumored that he buried treasure on Sanibel and Gasparilla Islands and then built a prison on "Isle de los Captivas," or Captiva Island, where he kept his female prisoners captive for ransom (hence the name Captiva).

Early Pioneers

In 1870, the U.S. Government ruled that Sanibel Island would become a lighthouse reservation and, on August 20, 1884, the Sanibel Lighthouse was first lit; it remains a working lighthouse to this day.

The area near the lighthouse was once the center of island activity, where most of Sanibel's early pioneers passed through. By 1889, there were twenty-one houses and forty families living on Sanibel Island. In 1892, with a population nearing 100, Sanibel built its first schoolhouse, which visitors can now see displayed at the Sanibel Historical Village.

As wealthy industrialists from the north, such as Thomas Edison and Henry Ford, discovered the winter paradise of Fort Myers, they also managed to take boat trips to Sanibel Island for rest and relaxation.

In 1928, a dock was built at the east end of Sanibel, near the lighthouse, and ferry service provided transport to the island for the next thirty-five years. Sea captains and farmers quickly started to homestead the island. A village developed at Wulfert (near today's J. N. "Ding" Darling National Wildlife Refuge), where settlers planted grapefruit, watermelon,

Punta Rassa.
A flat point of land at the southern edge of the Caloosahatchee River, in decades past, Punta Rassa was peopled by fishermen, soldiers, cowboys and leading sportsmen from around the world. The steamboat *Gladys* carried mail, passengers, and freight from Fort Myers to Punta Rassa and the Gulf islands. Shown is the Punta Rassa Grocery that served the few residents living there and customers waiting for the ferry to Sanibel Island. *Circa 1960s, $3-5.*

Sanibel Island Gulf Shoreline.
The fertile sea and its shores helped provide the Calusa Indians with natural bounty. However, the sea also provided them with uninvited visitors—the Spanish conquistadores. Today, very little remains of the Calusa culture. Some physical remains of the Calusa Indians mound and canal-building society can still be seen on Sanibel and Captiva, but their major towns were on Pine Island, Mound Key, and other nearby Islands. One such site on Sanibel is the Wightman Site near Wulfort. In 1974 archaeologists examined environmental characteristics and artifacts from the Wightman Site and confirmed that early Indians occupation dated to 300 B.C. There are several large shell mounds, overgrown by vegetation, along the Shell Mound Trail in the J. N. "Ding" Darling National Wildlife Refuge. These Calusa Indian mounds were built of discarded shells and fish bones, but they were not simply refuge heaps. The mounds provided the people with elevation in their low-lying land. Leaders ruled from the mounds and the population could find refuge on them from storms and floods. Today two of the mounds have an elevation of nine feet and one mound is six feet tall. *Author photograph.*

and vegetable farms. Island agriculture never recovered from the hurricanes of 1921 and 1926, but a new source of revenue emerged—tourists.

Famous Americans continued to seek a tranquil retreat on the islands. President Teddy Roosevelt and poet Edna St. Vincent Millay visited the islands. Charles Lindbergh and his wife, Anne Morrow Lindbergh, were frequent visitors and Anne wrote her famous *Gifts from the Sea* while vacationing on Captiva Island. Jay Norwood "Ding" Darling discovered Sanibel on a trip in 1935. A Pulitzer Prize winning political cartoonist and noted conservationist, "Ding" wintered on Captiva for years to come and actively campaigned for federal protection of the island's fragile ecosystem. In 1945, more than 6,300 acres of mangrove, bay, and estuary became the J. N. "Ding" Darling National Wildlife Refuge, and today is home to more than three hundred species of birds, fifty species of reptiles and amphibians, and more than thirty types of mammals.

Bottom left: Automobile Ferry to Sanibel and Captiva Islands.
Val and Babe sent this postcard to Mr. and Mrs. John Schmidt in St. Louis, Missouri: "We have had a lovely four days at Fort Myers, was wondering if John ever visited this island, while he was down here. Starting north, today, would rather stay, Bye for now." *Cancelled 1957, $6-8.*

Below: Island Transportation.
In the beginning, there was a ferry. As early as 1925, residents, visitors, and their automobiles rode a daily ferry to Sanibel Island. If they missed the last 5:30 ferry back to Punta Rassa on the mainland, they instantly became overnight guests. This ferry service was provided by the Kinzie Brothers Steamer Line; steamboats also ran from Fort Myers to the nearby island communities. The fare was $1 for car and driver and 35¢ for additional passengers. Leon Crumpler was a ferry boat captain on the Kinzie Brothers Steamer Line for forty-two years. All supplies and mail arrived by the ferry. Longtime residents remember the excitement of going off the island to middle and high school on a ferried bus and the careful planning that went into a trip to Fort Myers to take care of chores and medical needs. Ferry service ceased with the completion of a causeway in 1963. Circa 1940s, $6-8.

Tarpon House Hotel in Punta Rassa. *Circa 1890s, $1-3.*

Throughout the 1950s and 1960s, Sanibel and Captiva's reputation as sanctuary islands attracted more and more visitors. Drawn by its now-famous beaches, shelling, fishing, and wildlife, visitors arrived via a half-hour ferry ride from Punta Rassa, near Fort Myers; $1 for car and driver, additional passengers 35¢. The Sanibel Causeway opened in 1963, resulting in even more tourists visiting the islands.

Near Right: Sanibel Island Causeway.
This $2.7 million automobile causeway, which connected Fort Myers at Punta Rassa with Sanibel and Captiva Islands, opened May 26, 1963. Motorists initially paid $3 (which remained constant for forty years) to cross the toll bridge toward Sanibel Island, and a drawbridge allowed boat traffic to pass—110,000 vehicles passed over the bridge during 1964-65. *Circa 1963, $4-6.*

Below: The Need for a New Causeway to Sanibel.
Between 2004 and 2007 the old drawbridge and bridges were replaced with a seventy-foot-high span and new bridges to Sanibel. The original Sanibel Island Causeway (shown here) serviced nearly 86 million cars during its 44-year tenure. More than 10,000 motorists cross the bridges most days, up to 12,000 in peak season. When the original bridge was built, Lee County Commissioners estimated it would accommodate a daily average of 577 cars. *Cancelled 1975, $4-6.*

Below Right: New Causeway Between Sanibel and Punta Rassa.
On June 28, 2007, Lee County celebrated the completion of a new causeway from the mainland to Sanibel Island. The new 2.7-mile, $137 million causeway brings throngs of sun-lovers to Sanibel's beaches for swimming, windsurfing, fishing, kite boarding, and picnicking. One of the old bridges has been reconstructed as a fishing pier. The new causeway welcomes visitors to the islands in a thoroughly modern style. *Author photograph.*

60

East End of Sanibel Island.
In 1884, the Sanibel Lighthouse first shone upon San Carlos Bay, warning sailors and cattle shippers away from treacherous sandbars. In 1928, the Kinzie Brothers constructed docks at the east end of Ferry Road, and from then until 1963, Ferry Road and Olde Town served as the hub of island guest activity. Olde Town Sanibel was located at the east end of the island, around the historic lighthouse. *Circa 1990s, $1-3.*

Sanibel Island.
Sanibel Island is approximately twelve miles long and four miles wide. This barrier island, just off Florida's southwest coast, is Florida's own Hawaii. Residents and visitors alike delight in Sanibel Island's salubrious tropical climate and its relaxing, laid-back lifestyle. Its brilliant sunrises and sunsets, fishing piers, and world-class shelling on miles of sugar-sand beaches keep bringing people back to the island. On Sanibel, people are fond of the old saying, "If God ever retired, He'd come to live on Sanibel Island." It has also been said that many residents, once they've arrived, yearn to bomb the causeway and fend off further settlers. Thomas Edison and Henry Ford, who were winter residents of Fort Myers, were frequent visitors to Sanibel Island to relax and enjoy the beaches. *Circa 1990, $1-3.*

SANIBEL

Our boat is drifting to the South
Upon the languid swell.
And through the dusk comes a welcome flash
From the light on Sanibel.

A silvery halo in the east
Promise of moonrise brings,
And in the dimness of the key
A mock bird, waking, sings.

The misty memory of a world
Where struggle is, and scars.
Floats by us like a shadow,
And is lost among the stars.

We drift, quiescent, to the South
In the enchanted spell
Of moonrise promise in the east
And the light on Sanibel.

Seining — Casa Ybel, Sanibel, Fla.

Seining Mullet.
Occasionally the waters around Sanibel are thick with mullet—fishermen (shown) attempt to net the leaping grey fish. When they weren't hauling in the big seines, they basked in the tropical ambience and ate fish, birds, guavas, hearts of palm, and gopher turtles. *Circa 1908, $6-8.*

A Sanibel Island Poem. *Circa 1910s, $3-5.*

Sunrise on Sanibel Island.
Sanibel and Captiva Islands are a wonderland of lush tropical foliage framed by the aquamarine waters of the Gulf of Mexico. Sometimes referred to as "Florida's answer to Tahiti," these two islands offer visitors a unique getaway from big city life. The islands bring rest and relaxation to the frayed nerves of the business visitor, merchant, or professional person. Everyone enjoys the rising sun setting sun, or watching the moon rise over swaying palms. Sunrise is also the best time to look for shells on the islands. *Author photograph.*

The Lighthouse.
When the lighthouse was built, Sanibel Island was nearly uninhabited, and the keeper and his family had 670 acres of land set aside for farming. Unfortunately, the sandy soil wasn't good for growing much of anything... except children. One lighthouse keeper who served there for twenty-two years had thirteen children. *Circa 1920s, $4-6.*

Far Right: Around the Lighthouse.
The grounds and beaches around the lighthouse are lovely with white sand, sea grapes, and sea oats. The beaches are covered with shells and are popular for shelling and swimming. *Author photograph.*

Sanibel Island Lighthouse.
Sanibel Island Lighthouse is perhaps the most photographed structure on the island, and in 1974 it was listed on the National Register of Historic Places. Built in 1884, it is located at the far eastern tip of Sanibel Island, and is a carbon copy of the Cape San Blas Lighthouse in the Florida Panhandle. The lighthouses on the Gulf coast are far apart. The Sanibel Island Lighthouse is the last one heading south until Dry Tortugas in the Florida Keys, 130 miles away. In 1949, the 102-foot-tall lighthouse was automated with a modern light beacon. *Circa 1940s, $3-5.*

Left Column:

Driftwood, Shells, and Fishing Pier.
The fishing pier, situated on the east end of Sanibel near the lighthouse, faces toward the causeway on San Carlos' Bay. Many varieties of fish are caught here, where the water is deep and the tide runs swift:

One of Sanibel's Favorite Creatures.
Looking out over the glistening water, one may catch a glimpse of a rolling gray fin slicing through the waves as they surface for air. Continued watchfulness may result in the sighting of one of the island's favorite creatures, the bottle-nosed dolphin. The dorsal or back fin keeps the dolphin moving in a straight line. As marine mammals, they require a tremendous amount of food in order to maintain their body temperature and metabolism. It is estimated that an adult dolphin eats about forty pounds of fish each day. The dolphins around Sanibel grow to an average length of eight to ten feet and weigh around 800-1,000 pounds. Their long, narrow, torpedo shape makes them ideally suited for life in the water. A dolphin propels itself with powerful up and down strokes of its tail. The flippers help the dolphin steer. They have excellent eyesight both above and below water. In the waters of the Gulf of Mexico, dolphins easily find sufficient food. *Circa 1990s, $1-3.*

Birds of Sanibel.
Over 300 species of birds either inhabit or visit this coastal barrier island. In fact, this area is considered one of the top birding destinations in the world. The J. N. "Ding" Darling National Wildlife Refuge and the Sanibel-Captiva Conservation Foundation are excellent examples of the island's varying ecosystems and contain lots of birds and wildlife; some of the stunning birds found on Sanibel are Roseate spoonbill (shown), great egret, osprey, white ibis, anhinga, pelican, moorhen, snowy egret, little blue heron, cormorant, and great blue heron. *Circa 1960s, $2-4.*

Right Column:

Gopher Tortoise Crossing.
Gotta love an island that posts gopher tortoise walkway signs on its busiest street, Periwinkle Way. Distant relatives of the sea turtle, gopher tortoises sometimes colonize in the dunes with their woodchuck-like burrows; however, they want no part of the sea. Gopher tortoises weigh about four pounds and travel about by day, sometimes on a roadway. *Author photograph.*

Food for Birds and Fish.
Shells and their inhabitants play an important role in island ecology. They help keep the sand neatly in place and restock the beaches with more as they're crushed by waves and other forces. They provide food for birds and fish. The scavenging and filtering performed by certain mollusks help cleanse Gulf waters. This great blue heron is looking for his next meal on Sanibel. *Author photograph.*

West Indian Manatee.
West Indian manatees, also known as sea cows, graze on the sea grasses surrounding Sanibel. Despite their size, they are extremely sensitive to cold water. During the warmer months, these gentle creatures are dispersed throughout the area, but in cooler weather, they congregate around warmer waters found around springs and the power plant east of Fort Myers. Floridians have protected this friendly animal as far back as 1892, when it became illegal to kill a manatee. *Author photograph.*

64

Shelling

Sanibel Island is notable for the number and variety of seashells on its beaches. Every tide and storm washes ashore thousands of specimens of some three hundred varieties. Among them are:

- the multicolored calico shells, of which the pale lemon-yellow is the rarest;

- the lion's paw, a dark orange-red;

- the white, bowl-shaped, yellow-lined buttercup, which comes from deep water and is seldom found in pairs;

- the delicately scalloped rose cockle, its interior shading from pale salmon pink to deep rose and often tinged with orange and purple;

- the large red-brown cockle, used for souvenirs and in the manufacture of trays, lamps, and other objects; the fragile white angel's wings;

- the Chinese alphabet, a smooth white shell with curious markings;

- the slender polished olive, tapering at both ends and shading from dark brown to light tan, also called the Panama shell.

- One of the rarest was the jumonia, a deep-sea mollusk, its creamy white exterior marked with spiral rows of square brown or orange spots.

Shelling on Sanibel Island.
The Gulf beaches of Sanibel Island run for twelve miles along its south face. Shelling is one of the biggest draws to Sanibel's beaches, with solitude on a well-preserved island finishing a close second. Sanibel Island has been deemed the best site for shell collecting in America and third best in the world; it's a popular destination for streams of tourists who have discovered it and neighboring Captiva Island. Tourists risk suffering shell shock just by visiting here. *Circa 1970s, $3-5.*

The Shell Coast.
With some 3,000 kinds of shells, Florida is a paradise for shell collectors, and not for nothing is the southwest coast known as the Shell Coast. Beaches here are encrusted with shells that are swept round the Gulf of Mexico and deposited along the shore. Sanibel and Captiva both jut out into the rich waters of the Gulf of Mexico and offer a natural catch-all for the billions of shells cast up during a storm or by tidal action. Breaking waves dredge up sand and shells and propel them onto the islands. There are about 275 kinds of shells found in the shallow waters of Sanibel and Captiva Islands. *Author photograph. Postcard, circa 1990s, $3-5.*

Top Row: The Sanibel Stoop.
The Sanibel Stoop, also known as the Sanibel Slouch, is the name given to the hunched-over position adopted by shell hunters as they shuffle along the beach. In the background is the Sanibel fishing pier. *Author photograph.*

A Cottage on the Gulf.
Casa Ybel Resort, located on the south beach of Sanibel Island, offers vacationers a relaxing spot to enjoy the water and sun. In the 1880s, Casa Ybel was known as "The Sisters." *Circa 1950s, $3-5.*

Early Tourist Shell Collectors.
By the time a small ferry boat for automobiles had been established in 1928, Sanibel had already become famous as a vacation spot for shellers. The abundance and variety of marine shells attracted scientists from the Smithsonian Institution and major northern universities. New discoveries led to the publication of scientific accounts and field identification books. *Author photograph.*

The First Shell Collectors.
Seashells have always dominated the lives and activities of most people who have lived on the island. Over a thousand years ago, the native Calusa Indians harvested millions of large whelks for food and used the emptied shells for tools and weapons. Many of the ancient village sites of these now-extinct people are built of mounds of these broken whelk shells. This image of Calusa Indian shell collectors is on display in the Bailey-Matthews Shell Museum on Sanibel Island. *Author photograph.*

66

Sixteenth Century Spanish Shell Collectors.
Explorers and fortune seekers from Spain and nearby Havana, Cuba, made frequent visits in the 1500s to San Carlos Bay to trade with the enslaved Calusa Indians. Often, souvenir shells were gathered from the beaches of Sanibel and Captiva. In lieu of elusive gold and pearls, the Spanish soldiers stocked up with water, deer meat, fish, and colorful seashells. As the area opened up to Spanish and later English settlers from the north, the island gained fame as a secluded haven for fishing, farming, and shelling. *Circa 1930s, $2-4.*

Shells from the Beach   Sanibel Island, Florida

Shells from the Beach.
Roy mailed this card from Sanibel to Miss Bernita Eddy in Freesoil, Michigan: "How would you like to be here with me and go shelling for some of these pretty shells. We had our Xmas here with Howard Miller's family. Going back to Venice tomorrow." *Cancelled 1954, $1-3.*

Nature's Gifts from the Sea.
Seashells are a natural, vibrant part of nature and come in two major categories. The univalve inhabits a single shell and includes such species as conchs and whelks. Bivalves and others including clams, cockles, and scallops live within two-hinged shells. The empty seashells that are found layered on the beach once were home to soft-tissue animals called mollusks. Mollusks build their shells by secreting a liquid that eventually hardens around them. As the animals grow, their shells grow with them. *Circa 1930s, $2-4.*

Seashells.
These shells came from the Shell Factory in North Fort Myers. *Circa 1960s, $1-3.*

A Sanibel Island Collection.
Some of the outstanding varieties in this collection are the Giant and Fighting Conch, Princess Helmet, Thorny Oyster, Measled Cowry, Giant Band, Lions Paw, Junonia, Tulip Band, Variegated Screw Shell, Angular Triton, Left-handed Whelk, and King's Crown. *Circa 1950s, $3-5.*

J. N. "Ding" Darling National Wildlife Refuge.

The largest and most accessible undeveloped portion of Sanibel Island is the 5,000-acre J. N. "Ding" Darling National Wildlife Refuge. The sanctuary was named for J. N. Darling, a famous political cartoonist who served as head of the U.S. Biological Survey. Under his supervision at least 330 wildlife refuges were established across the country. Through Darling's influence, a large tract of land was amassed from a confusing collection of owners willing to sell their properties and set aside as a refuge for migratory waterfowl. When President Harry Truman established the Sanibel National Refuge in 1945, it encompassed 2,392 acres on the bay side of Sanibel. Two years later, Truman proclaimed Sanibel Island as a sanctuary for migratory birds with more land added to the Refuge. In 1967, five years after Darling's death, the Refuge was renamed in his honor, the J. N. "Ding" Darling National Wildlife Refuge. It now encompasses more than 6,300 acres of wildlife habitat on and around Sanibel Island. *Author photograph.*

Observation Tower at Sunset.

Along the five-mile Wildlife Drive in the J. N. "Ding" Darling National Wildlife Refuge is this tower, which offers spectacular views of both salt and fresh water birds, other wildlife, and an overall cross-section of a mangrove community. *Circa 1990s, $1-3.*

Above: Bailey-Matthews Shell Museum.

The Shell Museum, located at 3075 Sanibel-Captiva Road in Sanibel, allows visitors a chance to uncover the secrets about the ocean over the past 15-20 million years, when most of Florida was ocean floor. This intriguing shell museum, which claims to display a third of the 10,000 shell types found in the world, gives some clues as to why people hit the local beaches in the first rays of dawn with hopes of spotting a brown speckled junonia, considered the rarest American shell found on Sanibel and Captiva beaches. *Author photographs.*

Above: Refuge Residents and Visitors.

The J. N. "Ding" Darling National Wildlife Refuge is used by nearly three hundred bird species, more than fifty types of reptiles and amphibians, and more than thirty kinds of mammals. Migrating warblers and other songbirds traveling the Atlantic flyway are regular visitors to the Refuge in spring and fall; during the winter months, white pelicans, blue-winged teal, red-breasted mergansers, and other birds make their homes here. Shown are the white pelicans, osprey, and Florida's favorite reptile, the alligator. *Circa 1990s, $1-3.*

Captiva Island, Florida

Captiva Island

In the 1930s, Captiva Island, reached by a bridge from Sanibel Island, was a Government lighthouse and quarantine station. President Theodore Roosevelt came here often for deep-sea fishing. A giant devilfish, or manta, measuring thirty feet across and weighing more than two tons, was landed by him after an all-day battle. Nearly fifty steel-jacketed, .30 caliber bullets were fired into the creature before it was beached on a small island in Blind Pass, which was afterwards called Devilfish Key. Roosevelt Beach here was named for the former President.

Left Column: Greetings from Captiva Island.
Directly north of Sanibel, Captiva is joined to her sister island by a fixed highway bridge. In many ways, Captiva is a carbon copy of Sanibel, except that it lacks the large wildlife refuges and is a bit less crowded. Captiva is five miles in length, but seldom more than a half-mile wide. The great hurricane of 1926 blew so much salt water over the island that the land was "ruined for agriculture." The laid back atmosphere provides a somewhat keyed-down Key West. Seashells have always influenced the lives of people on Sanibel and Captiva Islands. Anne Morrow Lindberg wrote the book *A Gift from the Sea* while living in a rustic cabin on Captiva. *Circa 1990s, $1-3.*

Aerial View of Captiva Island.
The northern tip of Sanibel Island is shown in the bottom right corner of this view. A sunken mid-1600s galleon lies in the Gulf of Mexico off the north shore of Captiva Island. The ship may have been blown ashore during a hurricane. Several Spanish Pillar Dollars have been recovered from the ship. Her remains could once be seen at low tide. Many Spanish coins have been recovered on the beach, which are assumed to have come from the galleon. *Circa 1990s, $1-3.*

Blind Pass Today.
Artist Robert Rauschenberg called Captiva Island home. Sometimes referred to as the "Father of Pop Art," Rauschenberg's spontaneous style was right at home on this laid back paradise island of beautiful beaches and quaint living style. *Circa 2003, $1-3.*

Top Right: South Seas Plantation Resort.
The South Seas Plantation Resort is located on the northern part of Captiva Island. This upper-crust establishment has a variety of accommodations including six hundred units, twenty-one tennis courts, nine-hole golf course, eighteen swimming pools, boat rentals, three restaurants, and lounge. *Circa 1990s, $1-3.*

Above: Bridge over Blind Pass.
Blind Pass separates Sanibel Island and Captiva Island. Shelling is very good on both sides of the bridge. *Circa 1960s, $3-5.*

Chapter Six:
Estero Island

Estero Island is a geologically young barrier island that was formed well after the end of the earth's last ice age. Florida's climate was cool and dry, and the peninsula was covered by grassy tundra. With sea level 150 feet lower than it is today, a south Florida Paleo Indian of 10,000 years ago who wanted to move his family to the beach would have walked west for about five days (more than seventy miles) just to get there!

Because of its proximity to the rich, food-producing estuaries of Estero Bay, Estero Island was once at the center of the Calusa Indian heartland. The Calusa paramount king, who the Spanish explorers called Carlos, ruled a vast South Florida empire from his ceremonial center on nearby Mound Key, a 125-acre island hidden deep in Estero Bay.

Fort Myers Beach

Fort Myers Beach is an eight-mile stretch of white sand on crescent-shaped Estero Island.

In 1893, Dr. Cyrus Teed (son of Jesse Sears Teed and Sarah Ann Tuttle) arrived on Fort Myers Beach. Teed's religious group, known as the Koreshan Unity, had established a settlement on the Estero River. Teed and his Koreshans, who believed that the earth was a hollow sphere, purchased large amounts of land on the mainland, as well as at Mound Key and on Fort Myers Beach. Teed died around the turn of the twentieth century and was buried on Estero Island.

In the 1930s, the beach was used as a motor highway bordered with cottages, small hotels, apartment houses, and a tourist camp. Boats, guides, and all equipment for surf and deep-sea fishing were available at the casino and many fish houses.

On the island was a plant canning coquina and turtle soup. Turtles were brought from interior points. The coquina, also known as the donax or pompano clam, a tiny mollusk seldom longer than half an inch, was found in great quantities at the surf line on Florida beaches. Standing on end, they burrow into the sand as each wave recedes. Their shells of infinite color and variety of markings were used in the preparation of shellflowers, butterflies, and other novelties sold in curio shops. The broth, served hot or chilled, was a great delicacy and one of Florida's popular native dishes. At Christmas celebrations held on the beach, a barefoot Santa Claus stepped from a speedboat and distributed gifts to island children under the coconut palms.

Top: Fort Myers Beach.
Sixteen miles from Fort Myers on Estero Island lies a seven-mile expanse of silver sand known as Fort Myers Beach, a popular resort colony complete in itself. Free from undertow, it is one of the safest beaches in Florida. The turquoise Gulf waters and white sand beach invite swimming, boating, fishing, sunning, and relaxing. For decades, tourists have been coming to this tropical getaway. The island began its transformation from a fishing village into a destination when World War II soldiers based at Buckingham Air Field and Page Field sought R&R on balmy Fort Myers Beach. After the war, those soldiers returned as tourists or residents. Motels, rental units, housing, restaurants, bars, and retail shops began to multiply. *Circa 1990s, $1-3.*

Right: Looking South on Fort Myers Beach.
This view shows the high-rise bridge connecting Fort Myers Beach to Fort Myers. *Circa 1990s, $1-3.*

Left: Bridge to Fort Myers Beach.
Fort Myers Beach, located on Estero Island, is connected to Fort Myers by bridge. In May 1921, cars crossed the wooden lift bridge to Fort Myers Beach at 50¢ a car. The take for the first day was $53. Today the island is connected to the mainland by a high-rise bridge. This view is looking north on Fort Myers Beach. *Circa 1950s, $3-5.*

Fort Myers Beach — Gulf of Mexico, Florida   FM-120

F.3—Bathing in the Gulf of Mexico on Beautiful Fort Myers Beach, Fla.

Left and Above: Bathing in the Gulf of Mexico.
Swimming, shelling, and sun can be enjoyed daily along Fort Myers Beach. Everyone enjoys the morning daredevil aerial show provided by the sea gulls and pelicans, as well as the more dignified ballet of the herons and ibises, some of which are the size of wild turkeys. The former dive-bomb the water, crashing headlong into the surf and disappearing from view, only to resurface seconds later with some squirming varmint in their beaks. *Postcard, circa 1940s, $3-5. Closeup of Heron, Author photograph.*

Beach Scene.
J. W. Chan sent this postcard of Fort Myers Beach to Dolores in Riverview, Florida. *Cancelled 1958, $3-5.*

F.30—Tropical Fort Myers Beach, Fla.

The Water's Fine.
These couples getting wet in the inviting waters of the Gulf of Mexico, revealing far more wet bathing costumes than suntan in the early 1900s. *Circa 1910, $4-6.*

A Day at the Beach.
Blue skies, white sand, warm Gulf of Mexico waters, and tropical coconut palms combine to make this a tourist paradise. *Circa 1940s, $4-6.*

Above: Aerial View of Lovers Key.
Lovers Key sits on Black Island, the barrier island south of Fort Myers Beach's Estero Island. The beaches on Lovers Key are some of the wildest and visually most interesting on Florida's southwest coast. In 1998, this area became known as the Lovers Key State Recreation Area, one of the nicest and newest of Florida's state parks. Shown are Lovers Key and the causeway that connects it to Fort Myers Beach (in the center). *Circa 1990s, $1-3.*

Right: The Mound House.
The Mound House, the oldest standing structure on Estero Island (Fort Myers Beach), sits atop a Calusa Indian shell mound constructed between 2,000–1,400 years ago. Archaeological evidence suggests the site may have been occupied during the sixteenth century Spanish discovery period and Cuban fisher folk in the 1800s. *Author photograph.*

Left: Kids Enjoy Playground at Fort Myers Beach.
Copyright 1958, $3-5.

Above: A Modern View of Fort Myers Beach.
Fort Myers Beach continues to draw hordes of tourists from all around the world. Shown is a drink cart vendor, complete with his palm tree designed cart, travelling past several sunbathing tourists. Within minutes, he was selling drinks to three of the tourists. Sandcastle building is also popular on this beach, especially in November when sand sculptors from around the country descend on Fort Myers Beach to create unbelievable sand castles. *Author photograph.*

Left: Fort Myers Beach Fishing Pier.
Fort Myers Beach's first fishing pier was built in the 1920s near today's library. Storms later blew it apart and, after a hurricane in 1944, a new 560-foot-long pier was built. *Circa 1990s, $1-3.*

Chapter Seven:
Pine Island

Pine Island is located just northwest of Fort Myers. Skeleton remains that date back to about 6,000 years have been unearthed on this island. The Calusa Indians also inhabited the island from 300 A.D. until the Spanish explorers arrived in the sixteenth century. In the early 1900s, there was a Seminole Indian village on the island.

Seminole Indians on Pine Island. *Circa 1900s, $5-7.*

Seminole Indian Mothers and Babies. *Circa 1930s, $3-5.*

Pine Island.
The largest island on the west coast of Florida, Pine Island is considered by many residents as the last fragment of Old Florida. It's sheltered to the west by the islands of Sanibel, Captiva, and Cayo Costa. Pine Island remains largely untouched by past and modern day building booms because it has no significant beaches. Located a few miles west of Fort Myers, it's a combination of five small communities: Matiacha is at the bridge that provides access to the island; Pine Island Center was originally known as Tom's Town for Tom Phillips, who planned it during the 1940s; Bokeelia in the north, Pineland in the western central area, and St. James City on the south end. *Author photograph.*

Pineland

The Calusa Indians were once the most powerful people in all of South Florida. For many centuries these Native Americans built huge shell mounds, engineered canals, and sustained tens of thousands of people from the fish and shellfish found in the rich estuaries west and south of Fort Myers. The Pineland area was a principal location of these ancient people.

The Pineland Archaeological Site complex is located in Pineland. The site was a Calusa Indian village for over 1,500 years. Enormous shell mounds still overlook the waters of Pine Island Sound. The remains of fifteen centuries' worth of Indian life are evident everywhere. Remnants of an ancient canal that reached across Pine Island sweep through the complex. Sand burial mounds stand in the woods. Native plants and animals characteristic of coastal hammocks, pinelands, wetlands, and Indian shell mounds are in abundance. Historic structures representing Florida's early pioneer history also still exist at Pineland. Archaeologists have been conducting research here since 1988. The site is listed in the National Register of Historic Places.

The Randell Research Center (RRC) is a permanent facility dedicated to learning and teaching the archaeology, history, and ecology of Southwest Florida. Situated in the scenic community of Pineland, the RRC encompasses more than fifty acres at the heart of the Pineland Archaeological Site, a massive shell mound extending across more than two hundred acres from the mangrove coastline. The Randell Research Center, part of the Florida Museum of Natural History (located on the University of Florida Campus in Gainesville), operates the Calusa Heritage Trail, a 3,700-foot walkway through this internationally significant site. The interpretive path leads visitors through the mounds, canals, and other features of the Pineland Archaeological Site and signs along the trail provide visitors with detailed information regarding the Calusa Indians, their culture, and their environment. The trail also features observation platforms atop the site's tallest shell mound.

Near Left: Pineland Archaeological Site.
The Pineland mounds formed a complex of pyramids and other elevated surfaces that are believed to have possessed religious significance. A large canal excavated by the Indians connected this site with the other side of Pine Island. In 1895, archaeologist Frank Cushing visited Pineland, then known as Battey's Landing, and other important sites, including Key Marco (Marco Island). He returned to Marco Island the following year and unearthed many important artifacts and wood carvings, and these are the most important remnants of Calusa civilization discovered to date. These Indian mounds often provided early white settlers with a convenient source of road fill, and many mounds have been lost to this process, including much of the Pineland site. The mounds also provided high and dry building sites and tend to be preserved when used in this fashion.

In 2004, Florida had a fierce hurricane season. Four major hurricanes destroyed property all over the state. Trees were blown down, and shell and burial mounds took a beating at Pineland. Archaeologists at the site, however, noted that the removal of trees has restored the landscape to its Pre-Columbian state, offering the same view a Calusa chief would have had from the mounds to the Gulf of Mexico. *This painting appears in the Calusa Indian exhibit at the Florida Museum of Natural History in Gainesville.*

Calusa Heritage Trail.
The 3,700-foot-long Calusa Heritage Trail is a walking trail featuring two enormous thirty-foot-high shell mounds, named Brown's and Randell, which look down upon the tranquil waters below. There is also the Smith Mound, a sand burial mound, and other visual pieces of historical structures that were once part of the Calusa Indians habitat. The trail is situated among remnants of a Calusa canal and shell mounds. *Author photograph.*

Above: Seminole Indian Village on Pine Island. *Cancelled 1912, $8-10.*

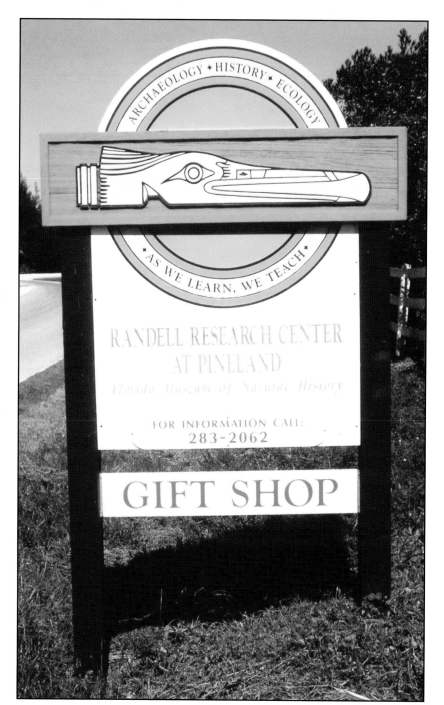

Near Left and Above: Randell Research Center.
Visitors to the 53-acre Randell Research Center can see what's been discovered about the powerful Calusa Indians. *Author photographs.*

Below: Pineland Post Office.
This Post Office is the island's smallest and oldest (circa 1927) building. A portion of the daily mail is picked up and delivered by a boat that services the many islands isolated from the mainland. *Author photograph.*

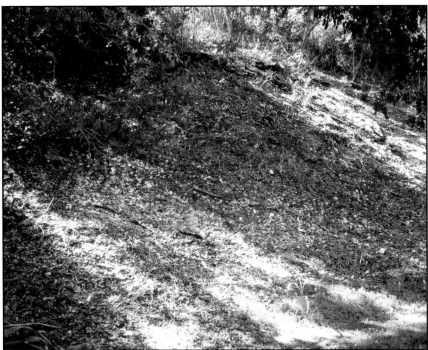

Brown's Mound.
Brown's Mound extended well over thirty feet. Its summit may have been the residence of the town chief and other nobles Pineland's residents probably also built houses on high places for practical reasons: protection from storm surges, biting insects, and human enemies. *Author photographs.*

What You'll See

The following ten images appeared on the interpretive signs along the Calusa Heritage Trail at the Randell Research Center in Pineland. The artist was Merald Clark.

Below and near right:
A Calusa Indian Community.

Perhaps a large Calusa community existed on and around Brown's Mound 1,500 years ago. The leader of the community may have had his house on top of Brown's Mound.

Bottom Right: A Special House.

In a small mound near Brown's Mound, archaeologists found evidence of a 700-year-old house. A dark layer suggests a house floor, and there is evidence of posts where walls once stood. The floor contained exotic materials, such as galena from Missouri. Galena may have also been used for body paint, suggesting that the house was used by high-status people to prepare for rituals. Archaeologists hope to excavate the remaining house features to learn more.

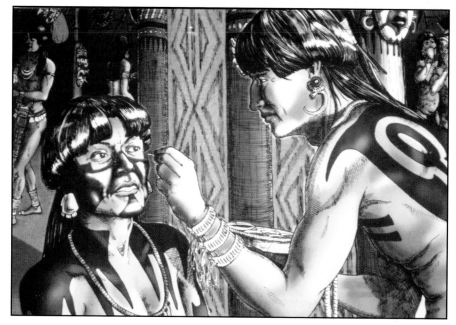

Above: A Life Shaped By The Sea.
The marine environment of the Calusa Indians was a profound influence in shaping their ideas, beliefs, skills, values, and knowledge. The Calusas made most of the abundant marine resources surrounding them. They dug canals to facilitate transportation, and sculpted canoes for carrying people, trade goods, and food. Tools, utensils, and vessels were made from shells. The shallow, accessible, productive estuarine bays appear to have produced enough food to sustain the people inhabiting adjacent shores and islands. As population increased, the Calusa Indians developed a variety of fish traps, weirs, and nets. On the basis of their success in fishing, the Calusas developed increasingly complex political and social structures.

Top and Near Left : Calusa Indian Tools.
When the worked conch or whelk shell has a beveled edge, the tool is called a cutting-edged tool. The lightning whelk was used to make chopping tools, chisels, adzes, and gouges. The sturdy lip of the queen conch were removed and then shaped into an axe-like tool called a celt. Celts were used to cut and shape wood. Tools were often hafted, or secured, to the shell with rawhide or cord. As the cutting-edged tool became worn from use, it was often reworked into a hammer or similar blunt-edged tool. Whether hand-held or hafted, blunt-edge tools were found in almost every early Indian midden. Shell hammers had working surfaces blunted from repeated use. Pounders were large gastropod shells with their outer whorls knocked or worn off.

Canal Dug and Used by the Calusa People.

Calusa Indians Cooking and Eating A Meal.

Calusa Indian Slavery.
Between about 1704 and 1711, Yamasee and Creek Indians ravaged South Florida in search of Indian slaves for sale to the English in Charleston, South Carolina. Boys and women of all ages were captured alive, while adult men who resisted were killed.

Below: Calusa Fishing.
Fishing was key to the Calusa Indians' survival, so they built trenches and canals to hold fish and use waterways. The Calusa Indians were expert fishers, and shells played a part in their success. Shell weights helped to anchor nets, and shell sinkers held fishing lines steady. Rectangular shell tablets, made from the whorl of a whelk, served as net gauges during the weaving of nets to assure even mesh sizes. Reels, made by chipping away opposite sides of a clam shell to form notches, could hold cordage or fishing line. Shark's teeth were used to create fishing gear. Calusa fishing also depended on materials from land, such as deer bone used to make throat gorges, fish hooks, and spear points. Nets were made of palm fiber. Canoes and traps were made of wood and vines. In one view, the Calusa Indians are pulling a seine net—this was one way they gathered fish for their next meal.

Bokeelia

A rustic and secluded village of fishermen and retirees, Bokeelia is located on the north end of Pine Island. For nearly twenty years the pirate Bru Baker and his crew of cutthroat men based their operations out of Bokeelia. Then in 1819, there were rumors that the United States was about to purchase Florida form Spain, and Bru decided to move his pirating operations.

Some of the best tarpon fishing in the world lies just north of Bokeelia, in Boca Grande Pass. Other popular game fish in these waters include snook, trout, redfish, cobia, sheephead, and grouper. Hence, the area around Bokeelia is a fisherman's paradise.

Bokeelia.
Old-time Florida houses and narrow streets crisscross the north end of Pine Island in the community of Bokeelia. Main Street is where the (little) activity occurs in this community. The waterfront atmosphere offsets the hustle and bustle of bigger city life. Bokeelia is a popular fishermen destination. *Circa 1990s, $1-3.*

Private Pier in Bokeelia.
Dick sent this postcard of Bokeelia to Mr. & Mrs. Eugene Channell in Spring Valley, Ohio: "We are at Ft. Myers Beach and soaking up some of the sun. Hope we can bring some back with us. Weather has been good on shore. We went out party boat fishing and the waves were pretty bad. Poor June and Jeff were so sick and we caught very little. It was so bad they refunded $4 of the $6 fee. We will see you all soon." *Cancelled 1970, $2-4.*

St. James City

St. James City was settled in 1887 by a group of wealthy New Englanders who constructed buildings of spruce and white pine shipped from Maine. Later the San Carlos Hotel was built and St. James City became a popular South Florida resort. After the death of the principal owner, the resort deteriorated and was later purchased by a sisal hemp company. The new owners rebuilt the town, erected a large factory for the manufacture of rope, and planted hundreds of acres in sisal, but the project was not a success and was eventually abandoned. In the 1930s, the settlement had a post office, school, general store, nursery, several fish houses, and a population of ninety people. Steamboats from Fort Myers stopped on the island twice daily on their way to other coastal resorts.

The steamer *Gladys,* of the Kinzie Brothers Steamer Line in Fort Myers, served the nearby islands, including Pine Island, from 1911 to 1936; it carried passengers, U.S. mail, freight, and crates of fruit and vegetables. The *Santiva,* a small gas-powered boat owned by the Singleton Brothers, made a daily run to St. James City from 1936 to 1952. During the sixteen years the Singleton Brothers, Ray and Cleon, ran the mail to Sanibel, Captiva, and St. James City, they were never late getting back to Fort Myers.

Just like the Calusa Indians, the Spanish conquistadores, the infamous pirates, the Seminole Indian village, and the fishing villages on Pine Island, the steamboats and gas powered boats vanished, leaving only memories for those who were fortunate enough to have plied these waters aboard their decks.

Museum of the Islands.
The Museum of the Islands is housed in what was once Pine Island's only public library. After the library relocated, the building became a museum. The purpose of the museum is to educate tourists and locals about the history of Bokeelia, Pine Island, and neighboring islands. Exhibits highlight the early fishing villages and inhabitants of the islands. *Author photograph.*

Chapter Eight:
Mound Key

One of Pre-Columbian Florida's largest and most complex architectural sites, Mound Key is located in Estero Bay, fourteen miles south of Fort Myers. The Calusa Indians created this 133-acre island over 2,000 years ago. Most of the island has been designated the Mound Key Archaeological State Park and is a detached portion of the Koreshan State History Site just across the bay in Estero. Of the 133 acres, 113 of those acres are managed by the park system. The State of Florida began acquisition of Mound Key in 1961.

Formation of the Island

The first Indians arrived on Mound Key about A.D. 100. The flat mangrove-and-oyster bar island barely rose above the shallow waters of Estero Bay. However, it was a good location to live as food was easy to come by. Fish were plentiful and, in the shallows around the island, oysters were there for the taking. Centuries rolled by with the collection of fishing and shellfish remaining at the core; as a result, discarded shells piled up and the island grew higher. As time went on, the residents reworked the accumulating shell middens, raising mounds and ridges, and carving out canals and water courts.

Researchers believe Mound Key was the site of Calos, the capital of the once-powerful Calusa Indian domain, which, as previously noted, included many of Southwest Florida's islands.

When Spanish explorers encountered them in the 1500s, the Calusa Indians ruled all of South Florida. Towns and villages throughout South Florida sent offerings of feathers, hides, fruit, mats, roots, and occasional Spanish captives to the Calusa king.

Pioneers on Mound Key

Toward the end of the nineteenth century, American pioneers began to settle on the island. Most of the pioneers, like their Calusa and Cuban predecessors, made a living by fishing and oystering.

One group of settlers that made use of this indigenous-created island was the Koreshans, a communal society formed in Chicago and that established a utopian community by the Estero River in 1894. Eventually, they acquired portions of Mound Key, which sits at the mouth of the Estero. Many of Mound Key's residents moved to the mainland after the devastating hurricanes of 1920 and 1926. In 1961, with their numbers dwindling, the last Koreshans donated their property in Mound Key and Estero to the State of Florida so that a historical and archaeological park could be established.

Researchers continue to examine the Mound Key site in order to establish a better understanding of ancient Calos and its remarkable architecture.

An Archaeological Timeline

1885: The first archaeological account of Mound Key came from A. E. Douglass who visited the area.

Late 19th Century: Clarence B. Moore and Frank Hamilton Cushing, notable archaeologists, both visit.

• John M. Goggin and his University of Florida archaeology students made several surface collections.

• Frank Johnson, who lived on the island, and his sons found a large number of Indian and Spanish artifacts, which are described in anthropologist Ryan J. Wheeler's book, Treasure of the Calusa.

1978: Clifford Lewis' research was primarily directed toward the historical aspects of the early Spanish missions to the Calusas.

1983-Present: Archaeologist William H. Marquardt has directed an interdisciplinary project investigating the Calusa Indian people of southwest Florida and their Pre-Columbian ancestors.

1994: The work of Corbett Torrence included mapping and controlled surface collections, plus some limited excavation.

• Clifford Lewis, civil engineer James Marshall, and archaeologist John Beriault made maps of the mounds and other topographic features at Mound Key.

Florida Museum of Natural History. This museum is Florida's official Natural History Museum. The museum's two main facilities are located in Gainesville on the University of Florida campus. It is the largest collections-based natural history museum in the Southeast, with one of the nation's top natural history collections. One of the museum's permanent exhibition halls is dedicated to the people who have lived in South Florida through time and the environments that have supported them, including the Calusa, Seminole, and Miccosukee Indians. On display are more than 700 objects ranging from everyday items such as Calusa shell tools and fishing gear to thousand-year-old artifacts from archaeologist Frank Hamilton Cushings 1896 excavations at Key Marco (Marco Island). Also featured are Calusa Indian houses, shell mounds, and models of Calusa leaders. One of the most interesting exhibits is the museum's 1564 interpretation of the great Calusa Indian leader Carlos and his royal court at Mound Key. The museum also operates the Randell Research Center on Pine Island. *Author photograph.*

Capital of the Calusa

The eleven images contained in this section are part of the Calusa Indian exhibit at the Florida Museum of Natural History in Gainesville, Florida.

The Calusa king, or cacique, ruled his far-flung domain from an island town known as Calos. It was at Calos that the king, as ruler of South Florida, received the Spanish colonial governor, Pedro Menendez, in 1566. In 1567, the Jesuits founded a short-lived mission, San Antonio de Carlos, at Calos in a vain attempt to convert the independent-minded Calusa Indians. Researchers believe the town of Calos stood on Mound Key and here is how they described the island:

> "High on Mound 1, the king's house towered above the town. Across the central canal, in the court of the king (Mound 2), the Jesuits built their mission. To the northeast, on Mound 3, stood the Calusa temple. And all around the island, on shell ridges and high spots, were the houses of the people who lived at Calos. As many as 1,000 Calusa people once lived in Calos."

Mound Key has fascinated historians and archaeologists for many years. Using the mounds on the island, archaeologists have been able to piece together the story of the Calusa Indians, and they determined that ancestors of the Calusas used an array of hand-woven nets—gourd net floats, stone and shell net weights, and a host of other specialized tools—to collect in quantity everything that swam or crawled below the surface of the water.

The Calusa Indians.
The Calusa Indians were a powerful fisher-hunter-gatherer society with a complex political and military order normally found only among the settled Indians who raised crops. The name of the tribe derived from Carlos (Spanish equivalent of Calos), the name of their principal town or province as well as the name of their cacique or chief. *Drawing by Merald Clark.*

Carlos and His Royal Court.
This diorama represents a 1564 interpretation of the great Calusa Indian leader, Carlos, and his Royal Court at the Calusa island capital of Calos (today called Mound Key). The Royal Court consisted of (from left to right) Felipe, the Calusa military leader; Antonio, Carlos' sister, who was baptized Antonio by a Spanish priest; Tequesta, a visiting cacique from Southeast Florida; the Cacica, Carlos' young Queen, the first among his several wives; Carlos, King of the Calusa people; and Carlos' father (arm and leg shown), Head Shaman. This diorama was created by a group of people at the Florida Museum of Natural History that included the archaeologist, designers, and artists William Marquardt, Darcie MacMahon, Dorr Dennis, and Merald Clark. The lifelike figures were built in Vancouver, B.C. Their clothing represents information from records furnished by Spanish explorers who visited King Carlos' court during his reign.

Left: Carlos' Queen and First Among His Wives.
King Carlos' beautiful young wife as she appears in
the Royal Court diorama circa 1564.

Above: Carlos, King of the Calusa Indians.
The powerful leader of the Calusa Indians as he appears in the museum
diorama. In 1564, he was about twenty-three years old.

Near Right: Head Shaman.
The Shaman was the most powerful man in the
King's Court. The Calusa people believed he
could control the weather and the stars.

84

The King's Sister.
Antonio was the daughter of the Head Shaman and sister to King Carlos. She was formerly the King's principal wife.

The Calusa Military Leader.
War captain of the Calusas as he appears in Carlos' Royal Court circa 1564. Felipe was also brother to the queen.

Visiting Leader from Another Indian Tribe.
The leader of the Tequesta Indians, a tribe located in Southeast Florida, was a close relative of Carlos and Antonio.

King Carlos' Great Round House.
This palm-thatched structure was Calusa leader Carlos' house. This building was large enough for him to assemble up to 2,000 people. King Carlos' Royal Court was held in this house. *Drawing by Merald Clark.*

Two Leaders Meet.
In 1566, Calusa leader Carlos met Florida's Spanish governor Pedro Menendez in Carlos' house. The two leaders reached an alliance, but it did not last. *Drawing by Merald Clark.*

Far Right: Jesuit Mission, 1567-1569.
Spanish Jesuits established a mission at the Calusa capital town of Calos (now Mound Key) and attempted to make Christians of the Calusa Indians. But the Calusa remained true to their own beliefs, even after Spaniards killed their leader. The Jesuits abandoned the mission in 1569. *Drawing by Merald Clark.*

Last Days of the Calusas

Spanish governor, Fernandez de Olivera, wrote a letter dated October 13, 1612, in which he stated that during the past four years, half of the Indians had died because of the great plaque and other contagious diseases. European settlers brought their diseases with them, severely impacting the Indians, who had no natural immunity to them. They died in great numbers.

However, some Calusas were caught and sold as slaves. Whole villages disappeared, and by 1726, a small number of the greatly weakened Calusa tribe built a settlement near St. Augustine. No one knows what happened to the Calusa residents of Mound Key or exactly when they left, but by the eighteenth century, the island was home to several Cuban fishing families.

Some of the Calusa people may have lived on in South Florida, perhaps with newly arrived native peoples from the north, today known as Seminole Indians. In the 1930s, Smithsonian folklorist Frances Densmore collected Calusa songs among the Seminole Indians and said, "... that long ago the Calusa and Seminole camped near one another and the people of each camp visited freely in the other, learning songs and joining in the dances."

Chapter Nine:
Useppa Island

Its History

Useppa Island is a small island located in Charlotte Harbor at the northern end of Pine Island Sound. The island is long and narrow, approximately 1.02 miles long and 0.3 miles wide, its long axis running roughly north-south. A dune ridge runs from the northern end of the island to a point about two-thirds of the way to the southern end, then turns southwestward, ending near the island's western edge just north of the southern constriction. The southwest-trending portion of this elevated area is known today as "Calusa Ridge." Useppa has the highest elevation in Lee County because it was formed from the remains of a large sand dune created during the Pleistocene geologic period.

Paleo Indian people visited the island as early as 8000 B.C. From 5000-2000 B.C. Useppa Island served as a summer-fall fishing camp and columella-tool manufacturing area for Middle Archaic Indians. These people procured conch, clam, and whelks for food, wove plant fibers into nets for capturing fish, and made ingenious use of shells—especially lightening whelks—for tools, hammers, chisels, and containers. They also used their middens as places of burial. Potshards were found dating to 2020-1810

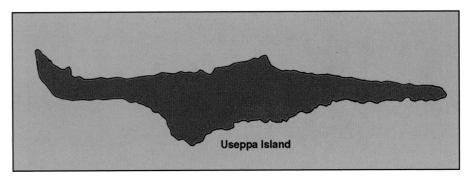

Useppa Island

Artist's Conception of Useppa Island.
Today the private island of Useppa is an upscale escape with world-class fishing. Fortunately, it does welcome the public during the day. Visitors can hop on a Captiva Cruise dining ship and see the island's small historical museum. The museum highlights the Indians that once inhabited the island. It also serves as a research point for the Florida Museum of Natural History. Circa 1920s. *Drawing by Author.*

B.C. within a midden containing clam and oyster shells and fish bones. Sharks, rays, pinfish, catfish, and sheephead were also commonly eaten. Plants used by these people included prickly pear, sea grape, acorn, hackberry, mastic, and panic grass.

Cuban Fishermen & the Military

In 1784 Cuban fishermen started using Useppa Island as a seasonal location for mullet fishing. Both Cubans and local Seminole Indians lived, fished, and farmed together in this activity. The fishermen continued using the island until the start of the Second Seminole War in 1835 when, fearing danger and removal, they left the island for Havana.

A supply depot on Useppa Island, called Fort Casey, was established in 1850 and garrisoned by 108 men. It was abandoned in November of the same year.

In 1863, during the Civil War, Useppa served as a staging area for Union soldiers and a point of refuge for citizens who were Union sympathizers. Union naval forces attempted, with mixed success, to seal Charlotte Harbor off from commerce. The main aim of the blockade was to prevent cattle deliveries to Confederate troops. A few farming settlements continued in the area and some may have provided fresh vegetables and fruits to Union soldiers. After the Civil War, Hispanic fishermen and traders reestablished themselves in Charlotte Harbor.

Archaeological Investigations

Jumping ahead to the late twentieth century, during the 1980s and 1990s, several archaeological investigations were performed on the island's shell middens. Thousands of artifacts were unearthed and studied during these archaeological digs.

In 1989, archaeologists discovered and removed a human burial located near the bottom of an archaic shell midden, and in 1994, the Useppa Museum opened. Its "Calusa Room" exhibits findings from the Florida Museum of Natural History's (at the University of Florida) investigations of 1985 and 1989.

Coconut Palm Trees on Useppa Island.
Circa 1902.

Useppa Inn

Useppa Inn.
John M. Roach bought Useppa Island in 1896 and constructed a winter residence there on an ancient Indian mound. Within a few years, he turned the home into the Useppa Inn, which became a popular residence for tarpon fishers. In 1907, the hotel's name was changed to the Tarpon Inn. In 1911, the island was bought by Barron G. Collier, an advertising millionaire who came to Southwest Florida from New York; he renovated the hotel, adding a beach and golf course. Over the years, the island has had several owners. Today the hotel is the Collier Inn. Shown is the side view of John Roach's Useppa Inn. *Circa 1902.*

Early People on Useppa Island.
Paleo Indians were the first people to occupy Useppa Island. An interesting Indian excavation can be reached by following the famous pink path running down the center of the island.

Barron Collier's Ownership

Barron Collier purchased Useppa Island in 1911, along with a boat and a mainland citrus grove, for $100,000. Collier added a nine-hole golf course, a 2,100-yard sand beach, an enlarged hotel, and a number of beach cottages.

Collier's Useppa Island was very successful in attracting the rich and the famous. Movie stars, sports personalities, prominent business people, and politicians were among those frequenting the island in the 1920s and 1930s. In 1928, the hotel's name was changed from Tarpon Inn back to Useppa Inn.

Barron Collier died unexpectedly on March 13, 1939 just ten days short of his 66th birthday. At the time of his death, he controlled an immense hotel, transportation, and communications empire and owned more than one million acres of land in Florida. The absence of Collier's energy and enthusiasm, coupled with increasing involvement of the country in World War II, led to a decision to close the island to visitors. The grand hotel fell into disrepair, suffered damage in a 1944 hurricane, and was demolished after the war. Collier's home, however, still stands today and is called the Collier Inn.

Useppa Island After World War II

The Collier family operated Useppa Island as a seasonal resort. Although there was no hotel on Useppa Island by the late 1940s, the island still welcomed seasonal tourists to its charming guest cottages. But activity on the island was relatively quiet compared to the "heyday" of the 1920s and 1930s.

In 1960, the Central Intelligence Agency used Useppa Island for secret training of officers for a planned Cuban invasion. Two years later William A. Snow purchased the island. He refurbished the buildings, installed a swimming pool, and built a septic system and an airstrip. In 1968, Jimmy B. Turner purchased Useppa Island, built new docks, and operated the island as a year-round resort for the first time. During the following years, the island changed hands several times.

Today, Useppa is a private island, but non-members can visit it in one of three ways: (1) as a guest of a member, (2) purchase a home or lot, or (3) traveling on a cruise boat that stops at Useppa Island for lunch.

Looking Toward Useppa Inn.
Visitors to Useppa Island have included President Theodore Roosevelt, Herbert Hoover, boxing champ Gene Tunney, author Zane Grey, and actresses Mae West, Hedy Lamarr, Shirley Temple, and Gloria Swanson. *Circa 1905.*

Chapter Ten:
Gasparilla Island

Charlotte Harbor and Northern Railway Passenger Depot.
Circa 1900s, $8-10.

A historical marker in front of the Depot reads: "On November 28, 1905, the steamboat *Mistletoe* of Tampa with the Engineer Corps and a force of 60 laborers landed on the beach directly opposite this spot, and the initial work of surveying and constructing the Charlotte Harbor and Northern Railway was commenced that day. This palmetto tree stood near the door of the officers' tent, and the glass insulators at the top of the tree are the original insulators that supported the wire of the first telephone line which was built on trees from Punta Gorda for the purpose of giving the headquarters of this company telephone communication."

Southern Tip of Gasparilla Island.
Gasparilla Island and Boca Grande was a fantastic and eye arresting spot that appealed to yachtsmen and sport enthusiasts. The Boca Grande Lighthouse is shown on the most southern tip in this view. *Circa 1940s.*

Scene showing S.A.L. Railway Station and Arrival of New York Special Tourists Train at Boca Grande, Florida

Railroad Station on Gasparilla Island.
Wealthy Northerners came to Gasparilla Island during the Roaring Twenties and thereafter to get away from the harsh northeastern winters. The quaint village of Boca Grande has long served as the center of activity on Gasparilla Island. Shown are the Seaboard Air Line Railway Station and the arrival of a New York Special Tourist train. Today visitors still find brick streets and walks flanked by cooling palm and banyan trees. The old Seaboard railroad depot has been converted into a complex of shops and a restaurant. *Circa 1930s, $8-10.*

Gasparilla Pirate Legend

According to Florida legend, the island was named after a pirate, Jose Gaspar, who based his operations from the island and supposedly hid his treasure there as well. The name "Gasparilla," however, appears on maps dated before the pirate's existence, casting doubt on the colorful legend.

In the late 1700s and early 1800s, the waters surrounding Florida were filled with brigantines, slave ships, bootleggers, merchants, and frigates from Spain, England, and the young United States... and pirates. The pirates were an early version of today's organized crime—with leaders, a strict code of honor, and their own form of government.

Legend has it that pirate Jose Gaspar, better known as Gasparilla, reigned in the Florida Keys and along Florida's West Coast from Marco Island to Tampa Bay. The barrier islands along Florida's Gulf Coast, the rivers, and harbors were a perfect location for international outlaws to establish a base of operations.

Jose Gaspar was born near Seville, Spain in 1756. Gaspar began his career as a lieutenant in the Royal Spanish Navy. In 1783, while serving on the *Florida Blanca*, Gaspar and his compatriot, Roderigo Lopez, led a bloody mutiny, captured the ship, and headed for the Florida Straits to set up business as pirates. During this journey, Gaspar changed his name to "Gasparilla." After reaching Florida, Gasparilla sailed up the West Coast, set up headquarters on one of the islands, and named it Gasparilla Island.

During the next twelve years, Gaspar looted and sunk thirty-six ships. He quickly became known as something of a local Bluebeard, and stories of his bloody raids struck a note of fear in both Spanish and American merchantmen.

Gaspar and his merry band of buccaneers dominated West Florida's coastal waters during the late eighteenth and early nineteenth centuries. The legendary pirate was a paradox of good breeding and low morals, prone both to bloodthirsty acts and surprising kindnesses.

Gaspar continued his pirating career for forty years. His downfall came in 1821, when he attempted to capture a United States warship, the *U.S.S. Enterprise*, in disguise. The battle was quickly over and Gaspar's ship was soon a burning wreck. It is rumored that rather than surrendering, Jose Gaspar wrapped himself in chains and jumped into the sea.

Early Settlers

The early settlers came to Gasparilla Island to fish. By the late 1870s several fish ranches were operating in the Charlotte Harbor area. One of them was located at the north end of Gasparilla Island in the small village called Gasparilla. The fishermen, many of them Spanish or Cuban, caught huge catches of mullet and other fish and salted them down for shipment to Havana and other markets. In the 1940s, the Gasparilla Fishery was moved to the town of Placida across from the Charlotte Harbor bay, where it still stands today, and the fishing village died out. Today, many of the island's early fishing families are still represented in third, fourth, and even fifth generation descendants who pursue many different vocations, including fishing.

Tarpon Fishing

Wealthy American and British sportsmen began discovering the Charlotte Harbor area for hunting and its fantastic fishing, notably for the worldclass game fish, tarpon. The silver-scaled tarpon ruled the turquoise Gulf waters in Boca Grande Pass, providing a sport fishing lifestyle unlike any other in the state. Nowhere else are tarpon as plentiful, and the Pass has become acclaimed as the "Tarpon Fishing Capital of the World."

Phosphate Rock Discovered

In 1885, phosphate rock was discovered on the banks of Peace River, east of Gasparilla Island, across from Charlotte Harbor toward Punta Gorda. It was this discovery that would turn the southern end of Gasparilla Island into a major deep water port (Boca Grande Pass is one of the deepest natural inlets in Florida) and become responsible for the development of the town of Boca Grande.

Phosphate was a valuable mineral for fertilizers, as well as other products, and was in great demand worldwide. At first, the phosphate was barged down Peace River to Port Boca Grande, where it was loaded onto schooners for worldwide shipment. By 1905 it was felt that building a railroad to Port Boca Grande and carrying the phosphate to it by rail should improve the method of shipment. The Charlotte Harbor and Northern Railroad was completed in 1907. For the next fifty years, phosphate would be shipped out of Port Boca Grande. Phosphate laden trains were often loaded directly onto ocean-going freighters, and the ships took the valuable commodity to ports all over the world. In 1969, Port Boca Grande ranked as the fourth busiest port in Florida. In the 1970s, phosphate companies switched their interest to other ports and the phosphate industry in Boca Grande came to an end by 1979.

Pirates and Gasparilla.
Who were the Pirates? Daring figures who swooped onto treasure ships and into remote cities, then returned home with golden cargoes? Brutal sea thieves who showed no mercy to their victims? Bold adventurers who financed travel by nautical theft? In fact, they were all these more—and one of the famous was the infamous Jose Gasper (aka Gasparilla). Legend has it that during the 1700s Gaspar established his headquarters in a small deep harbor at the north end of Gasparilla Island, located north of Captiva Island, between forays on the Gulf of Mexico and along the Spanish Main. Tall tales speak of his warehouse of treasures and ill-gotten booty. Gaspar and his band of corsairs supposedly used the island to stage nefarious raids against ships laden with booty. But the Spanish Gaspar was not always a pirate—he had stood in high favor at court until he stole a ship of the Spanish navy.
Records of Gasparilla's exploits were acquired from his brother-in-law, Juan Gomez. From 1784 to 1795 Gasparilla kept a diary in which he recorded his captures and the amount of plunder. In eleven years he captured and sank thirty-six ships. One entry was a census of the pirate band as follows: eight officers, forty-three able bodied seamen, twenty-three wives, twelve man servants, eight maidservants, sixteen probationary prisoners including seven men, six women, and two small boys. The band broke up in 1822 when Gasparilla gave chase to what appeared to be a large British merchantman; upon being overtaken, the vessel lowered the British flag, ran up the Stars and Stripes, and uncovered a masked battery. With his ship riddled, Gasparilla wrapped an anchor chain about his waist, and leaped into the sea. Ten of his crew were caught and hanged, but the few pirates ashore on the island escaped.

Boca Grande

Boca Grande, located on the southern end of Gasparilla Island, was named for the wide pass south of the island leading into the Gulf of Mexico; the natural harbor, with its six hundred-foot channel, is one of the deepest in Florida. For many years the village was a phosphate shipping point and a noted tarpon fishing community. A ferry was operated between Placida and Boca Grande.

The yellow-and-white wooden Gasparilla Inn, completed in 1912, along with a marina and nearby bathing casino, formed the popular resort. Wealthy northern families came by private Pullman cars attached to trains that ran the Charlotte Harbor and Northern Railroad line. The railroad station was built in what would become downtown; roads, sidewalks, shops, streetlights, a post office, and water and telephone service were not far behind. The town was landscaped. The railroad company built several cottages downtown and a few of the wealthy Northerners built winter residences. The train stopped at Gasparilla, the fishing village at the north end of the island; at the railroad depot in downtown Boca Grande; and at the south end phosphate terminal.

The Boca Grande Hotel was built in 1929, south of downtown Boca Grande. It was a three-story brick resort. Over the years the hotel had several different owners and was demolished in 1975.

Ferryboats and the railroad brought people to the remote island. The railroad continued to bring tourists to Gasparilla Island until the Boca Grande Causeway opened in 1958. The depot was restored in the 1970s and a number of offices, shops, and a restaurant now occupy the former Spanish-style railroad terminal.

Beach Scene at Boca Grande.
Tarpon fishing wasn't the only recreation found in Boca Grande. Island wanderers appreciated seven miles of barrier island beauty and tangerine sunsets. Shown is the beach directly in front of the Boca Grande Hotel, which afforded excellent year round bathing in the temperate waters of the Gulf of Mexico. *Circa 1930s, $1-3.*

THE BOCA GRANDE HOTEL — BOCA GRANDE, FLA.

Boca Grande - Florida

Gasparilla Island Lighthouse

The Port Boca Grande Lighthouse, originally called the Gasparilla Island Light Station, was built in 1890 at the southern tip of Gasparilla Island to mark the entry into Charlotte Harbor from the Gulf of Mexico. The Port Boca Grande Lighthouse, the oldest building on Gasparilla Island, is a one-story wooden dwelling on iron pilings with a black octagonal lantern on top. The lighthouse has survived several hurricanes. The U.S. Coast Guard abandoned it in 1967; in 1980, it was placed on the National Register of Historic Places. In 1986, the lighthouse was restored; in 1999, it opened to the public as the Boca Grande Lighthouse Museum.

About a mile northwest from the Port Boca Grande Lighthouse at the southern tip of Gasparilla Island is a tall, gangly, pyramidal structure with a black lantern 105 feet above mean sea level. It is called the Boca Grande Lighthouse; built in 1927, it still guides harbor traffic at night.

Boca Grande Lighthouse.
On December 31, 1890 a cottage-style lighthouse provided light out over the Gulf of Mexico for the first time, and storm-tossed sailors breathed a sigh of relief. In 1927, a second lighthouse was built on Gasparilla Island to serve as a rear range marker for the older light. This tall, white, skeletal structure still stands by the Gulf beaches near the village of Boca Grande. *Circa 1927, $3-5.*

Part III: Visiting Surrounding Communities

Chapter Eleven:
Naples

Naples is located on the Gulf Coast, thirty-five miles south of Fort Myers. The city is noted for its fabulous sunsets over the Gulf, a late day display of natural pyrotechnics. Naples occupies a long, slender point of land that thrusts between the Gulf of Mexico and the many canals of Naples Bay.

In the Beginning

Thousands of Calusa Indians and their ancestors once occupied the land now known as Naples and its surrounding communities. The Calusa Indians were a highly industrious tribe, often compared to the Incas and Mayans, who inhabited Southwest Florida for more than 2,000 years. But after defeating Spanish conquistadors, plagues of European diseases swept through the tribe, wiping out almost all of the Indians. Those who survived disease, warfare, and slavery are believed to have gone to Cuba. By the end of the eighteenth century, the Calusa Indians were all gone.

These Indians left mountainous shells mounds thus providing some evidence of where and how they lived. Shell mounds, consisting principally of clam, conch, and oyster shells, are found at hundreds of locations near Naples, including Marco Island, on almost all 150 acres of Chokoluskee Island, on many of the Ten Thousand Islands, and on sites in north, east, and south Naples. However, most of the mounds in Naples have been altered by construction projects, thus destroying much of the history of these ancient people.

Above: Sunset in Naples.
The coastal city of Naples is aptly called the Palm Beach of the Gulf Coast. It has been in the tourist business since 1887, placing it among the older resort cities. You need only a brief drive around the downtown area of fine shops and through some of the residential sections to realize that it's a place for the wealthy.
Naples is a seaside community and popular tourist destination on the Southwest coast, a few miles south of Fort Myers. It is famous for its fabulous sunsets. *Circa 1990s, $1-3.*

Left: Naples Pier.
The T-shaped pier was originally built in 1888. In spite of being rebuilt following a hurricane in 1910, a fire in 1922, and hurricane Donna in 1960, this venerable structure survives intact. The 1,000-foot pier remains Old Naples' focal point and is a popular gathering spot for fishermen, sunset gazers, strollers, pelicans, and dolphins. The fishers catch red snapper, grouper, snook and other regional species. Located at the west end of 12th Avenue South, it's Naples' famous landmark. *Circa 1930s, $3-5.*

MUNICIPAL PIER
& BATHING BEACH,
Naples, Florida

The Start of a City

Naples, named for the Italian city, was planned as a winter resort as early as 1887, when this part of Florida was still isolated and all mail and supplies had to be brought from Fort Myers by boat. A frame hotel and a few cottages were built, but Naples' growth was stalled by the lack of transportation. The construction of the railroad and the Tamiami Trail led to the building of a large tourist hotel and numerous cottages along the seven-mile stretch of white beach. Walter N. Haldeman, former publisher of the Louisville, Kentucky *Courier-Journal*, and 'Marse' Henry Watterson, editor of the *Courier-Journal*, were among the first settlers in Naples and aided in its development; Haldeman built the Naples Hotel in 1890.

In 1946, Henry B. Watkins, Sr., an Ohio manufacturer, and several partners acquired the hotel, along with 20,000 acres that constituted most of the undeveloped portions of Naples. After Hurricane Donna damaged the hotel in 1960, it was torn down and a new complex erected on thirty acres to the north. That hotel, now the Naples Beach Hotel and Golf Club, has been in the Watkins family for three generations.

Walter Haldeman built Palm Cottage in 1895 as a vacation home for his famous editor, Watterson, who spent many of his "working vacations" there. The home is one of the last tabby homes remaining in Southwest Florida.

In 1906, Watterson reported in the *Courier-Journal*:

"Naples is not a resort, but to the fisher and hunter, Naples is virgin; the forests and the jungle about scarce trodden the waters, as it were, untouched. Fancy people condemned to live on venison and bronzed wild turkey, pompano and sure enough oysters—and such turkeys! And such oysters!

"It is a sea-washed stretch of sandy beach, white as snow and gently firm, like paving asphalt, North to South from Doctor's Inlet to Gordon's Pass, 7 miles. Eastward, a trelliswork of orange groves, palm gardens, and orchards of coconuts, pineapples and mango, interlaced by tropic flora; to the west, an endless girdle of wave and sky. Midway, a long pier, with a group of cottages nestled about, and embowered in the setting a larger and more portentous edifice, technically described as a hotel, but looking he house of a gentleman. And this is Naples..."

Naples has long been known for its miles of shimmering white beaches lapped by gentle waves from the Gulf of Mexico. Travel publications regularly name the pristine beaches as among the best in the world for quality of sand, abundant shelling, and year-round swimming.

Naples Pier

Built in 1888 as a freight and passenger dock, the Naples Pier stands as a community landmark. Narrow gauge train rails spanning the length of the pier transported freight and baggage in the early 1900s. Part of the structure, as well as the post office that was located on the pier, was razed by fire in 1922. Rebuilt after damage from hurricanes in 1910, 1926, and 1960, it remains a public symbol of the area's history.

Waves from the Gulf of Mexico.
Back in the early 1930s, winter visitors came to Naples to enjoy the sun, the beaches and a small golf course located at the end of Fifth Avenue near the beach. It was in 1932 that Charles Lindbergh landed his plane in that area. Lindbergh and his wife, Ann, had a retreat in Sanibel Island and would drop in to pick up supplies. *Circa 1930s, $4-6.*

Naples Railroad Depot

The Naples Depot, which was completed in 1927, is one of the oldest remaining structures in the City of Naples. The Depot was built to serve as the Seaboard Air Line Railway's southernmost West Coast terminal. The coming of railroads to Naples and the opening of the Tamiami Trail in 1928 gave impetus to the growth of the area as a winter resort. The Naples Depot for a time became the property of the Atlantic Coast Line Railroad before a merger in the late 1960s brought it under the auspices of the Seaboard Coast Line Railroad.

It remained a hub of activity for tourists and residents for several decades. In 1971, increased reliance upon auto and air transportation resulted in the discontinuation of passenger service to Naples. Originally designed in a style compatible with the tropical Florida climate, the terminal building was added to the National Register of Historic Places in 1974.

M.143—Coconut Palms Line the Beach at Naples, Fla. on the Gulf of Mexico

The Fishing Pier, Naples, Florida

Left: Palm Cottage.
In 1895, Naples' businessman Walter Haldeman built a house for his good friend and business associate Henry Watterson, as an annex to the hotel he owned. The twelve-room house is built from mortar made with local shells, a mixture called tabby. Watterson, the editor of the Louisville *Courier Journal,* a newspaper owned by Haldeman, was a well-respected political writer whose editorials were syndicated throughout the country. Watterson died in 1902. When Haldeman died in 1916, the house was sold to the Walter O. Parmers. The Parmers named it Palm Cottage, adding indoor plumbing and, in 1926, converting it to electric power. Parmer died in 1932; his wife sold the house in 1938. After 1946 it became famous under the ownership of Laurance and Alexandra Brown. The Browns had a custom of raising a "cocktail flag" when the fun was about to begin. Robert Montgomery, Hedy Lamarr and Gary Cooper were entertained at Palm Cottage. The Collier County Historical Society purchased the house in 1979; Palm Cottage, the oldest house in Naples, was listed with the National Registry of Historic Places in 1982. *Author photograph.*

The Fishing Pier.
Nationally known watercolor artist Paul Norton painted this scene of the famous Naples Fishing Pier. *Circa 1940s, $3-5.*

Coconut Palm-Lined Beach at Naples.
The beautiful white sand Naples beach stretches more than seven miles along the Gulf of Mexico. *Circa 1940s, $3-5.*

Boaters, Swimmers, and Sun Bathers Relax at Naples Beach.
Circa 1960s, $2-4.

The Popular White Sand Beach, Naples-On-The-Gulf, Florida

NAPLES, FLORIDA

EDUCATED BIRDS PERFORM
4 WATER SHOWS DAILY

New! Caribbean Gardens

Exotic toucans are among the hundreds of rare birds and waterfowl that roam freely in this beautiful sanctuary.

Midway thru the Gardens, the friendly atmosphere of our Pavilion Restaurant invites you to relax and enjoy luncheon.

Feed the birds at Caribbean Gardens, Naples, Florida

Left and Above: Caribbean Gardens.
Famed botanist Dr. Henry Nehrling founded the Caribbean Gardens in Naples in 1919. The gardens were his dream tropical gardens where rare plants from all over the world could grow. Nehrling expanded his collection to over 3,000 plant species, but after his death in 1929, his gardens grew wild and untended for the next two decades. Julius Fleischman, grandson of the man who pioneered Fleischmann yeast, acquired the gardens, restored the site, added birds, lakes, and plants, and in 1954, opened it as Caribbean Gardens. In 1964, after Fleischmann's death, world traveler and expedition leader Colonel Lawrence "Jungle Larry" Tetzlaff and his wife, Nancy "Safari Jane" Tetzlaff, relocated their collection of rare and endangered animals to the gardens, renaming it Jungle Larry's Safari. It closed after thirty years in 1994, and the location reverted to Caribbean Gardens. Shown is Toni Blake feeding the birds from her own private lake at Caribbean Gardens. *Postcard circa 1955, $4-6; brochure circa 1955, $5-7.*

Naples Zoo.
This 1590 Goodlette-Frank Road location, where in the past Caribbean Gardens, Jungle Larry's Safari, and Jungle Larry's Zoological Park at Caribbean Gardens have been, is now home to the Naples Zoo. *Author photograph.*

Jungle Larry's Safari.
A self-guided trail wound through this preserve and botanical garden where wild birds and animals lived in a jungle-like setting. A short safari cruise took visitors to islands where primates lived in natural habitats. The park was one of the few places in Florida where visitors could view a rare collection of free-roaming primates, from spider monkeys to gibbons to lemurs. Cougars, hedgehogs, tiger, leopards, and wallabies could also be seen during the safari cruise and tram rides. Shown is "Kiki," a baby African Elephant. *Circa 1960s, $4-6.*

Chapter Twelve:
Bonita Springs

Bonita Springs is on the Tamiami Trail, eighteen miles south of Fort Myers. It is roughly halfway between Fort Myers and Naples.

In 1885, Braxton Bragg Comer, a wealthy Alabama farmer, and Archibald McLeod, his business partner and friend, came to the area seeking farmland. They bought 6,000 acres along Surveyor's Creek. Fifty workers and twenty-five mules cleared twenty acres and planted bananas, coconut palms, and pineapples. By 1893, the pineapple groves were flourishing, but that winter a bitter freeze destroyed the banana and pineapple plants. Other farmers came to the area and planted Orange groves. The area became known as Survey.

Panoramic Aerial View of Bonita Springs.
The beaches of Bonita Springs are now filled with high-rise luxury condominiums. On the mainland side, Bonita Springs and neighboring Estero to the north are bursting at the seams with mega-shopping centers. *Circa 2000, $1-3.*

A Town's Timeline

1887: A small, thatched-roof, log-walled public school was built.

1901: A Post Office was opened in the town of Survey.

1910: A frame two-story Eagle Hotel was in business catering to visitors who were attracted to the unspoiled area's bounty of hunting and fishing. By 1912, there were seventy students from twenty families enrolled in the public school.

1912: A group of investors, led by a Tennessean named J. Henry Ragsdale, bought 5,000 acres including Survey, which became Bonita Springs, named for Ragsdale's daughter, Bonita, and a local spring. At this time, transportation was mainly by steamboat.

1917: A barely passable road was completed between Fort Myers and Bonita Springs.

1923: The Fort Myers Southern Railroad reached Bonita Springs.

1928: Bonita Springs had a paved road that led south to Naples and east to Miami (Tamiami Trail). Bonita Springs was incorporated, churches were built, sawmills flourished, and a hotel was built. Tourist attractions were also established, delighting thousands of visitors year after year.

Tourist Attractions

Everglades Wonder Gardens

In 1936 the Piper brothers, Bill and Lester, built an attraction displaying alligators, cougars, other wild animals, and native plants. The attraction was called the Everglades Wonder Gardens, located on the Tamiami Trail (U.S. Highway 41), eighteen miles south of Fort Myers.

The Piper brothers had one of the biggest alligator and crocodile collections in Florida. They were especially proud of their crocodile pool, which included thirty-two crocodiles in one enclosure. Dynamite, a 14'3" long crocodile, was the king of the pool. In a separate pen was Big Joe, a twelve-foot long baddie that killed seven other crocodiles over a period of a few months in 1949. The alligator pool was full of large gators, scores of them ten to fourteen feet long; the Pipers caught many of them themselves in nearby Imperial River.

Today the gardens are one of Bonita Springs' largest attractions.

Welcome to Everglades Wonder Gardens.
The park opened February 22, 1936 and has been a member of the Florida Attractions Association since its beginning. The park has early 1930s animal housing that enables visitors to get up close to each exhibit. These animal enclosures are nested among a beautiful botanical garden. *1940s road sign, author photograph; brochure, circa 1940s, $3-5.*

Real Photo Postcard.
This RPPC is of alligators at Everglades Wonder Gardens. At the time this postcard was made, the roadside attraction had an All-Florida exhibit with 2,000 alligators, crocodiles, snakes, animals, and birds that taught visitors about life in the mysterious Everglades. *Circa 1930s, $8-10.*

Alligator Pool.
Circa 1930s, $2-4.

Crocodile Pit at Everglades Wonder Gardens.
Circa 1936, $4-6.

Shell Factory

Canadian Harold Crant saw the millions of shells lying free for the taking, knee-deep in brilliantly colored windrows along the beaches, and opened the Shell Factory in 1938. The factory burned down in the early 1940s, but was later rebuilt in North Fort Myers.

Naples-Fort Myers Greyhound Track.
On December 27, 1957, the race track became part of the laid-back Florida lifestyle and a stalwart of Bonita Springs. Everything was rustic around Bonita in the 1950s. People were a bit upset about the track being called the Naples-Fort Myers dog track when it was in Bonita. The track was popular during the 1960s-1980s. In 1997, the track opened a poker room with over thirty tables. *Author photograph.*

Naples-Fort Myers Greyhound Track

Bonita Springs also became the home of the Naples-Fort Myers Greyhound Track. This track, which also has a poker room, is open with a year-round schedule.

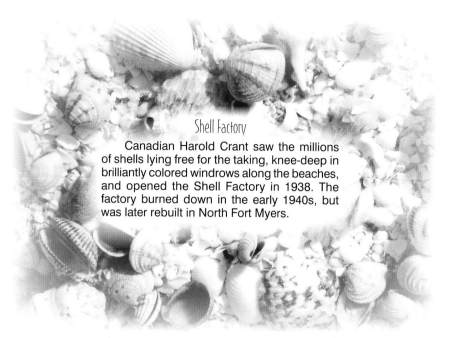

And They're Off!
"Going to the dogs" is a favorite pastime in Bonita Springs. *Circa 1980s, $3-5.*

Chapter Thirteen:
Marco Island (Key Marco)

The largest of Florida's Ten Thousand Islands, Marco Island is also the only developed island in this mangrove chain. A beachfront paradise located a few miles southeast of Naples, it is surrounded by the Gulf of Mexico on one side and pristine wilderness on the other. The island is also called Key Marco. One of the richest collections of carved and painted ceremonial and utilitarian aboriginal objects found in Florida was unearthed here by accident in 1896.

Today, Marco Island has some of the world's most beautiful beaches. Its platinum beaches bring vacationers to stay at high-rise resorts. Its proximity to the superb fishing, boating, shelling, bird and wildlife watching, kayaking, and canoeing in and around the Gulf, mangrove-lined estuaries, and the Everglades adds further dimension.

With the archaeological exploration of Key Marco far from complete, the islet (now known as Marco Island) is being transformed into a resort complex, which may forever bury the mystery of the past.

The Settlements

There were three settlements on Marco Island: Collier City, Goodland, and Caxambas.

Collier City

The first settler at Marco Island was W. T. Collier from Tennessee. He had eight children, the most prominent of whom was Captain William D. Collier. In 1927, when a New York syndicate promoted a big boom time development there, they got the Legislature to incorporate all of Marco Island as a city and named it "Collier City." Today, there is no such place as Collier City.

Goodland

Goodland is a tiny fishing village that refused to join the twentieth century. Located here is a massive, 68-acre Indian shell mound. Archaeologist John Goggin collected over 350 artifacts and nearly 5,000 pottery shards from the site in 1950. Today, the mound is covered with mobile homes.

Caxambas

A forty-acre shell mound, once located on the shore of Caxambas Pass at the south end of Marco Island, marked the place where the village of Caxambas once stood. The Calusa Indians began the formation of this shell mound nearly 2,000 years ago. Caxambas was one of the oldest place names on the coast and quite likely the oldest in Collier County. It appears on the William Gerard De Brahms Chart of Southern Florida in 1881 as "Caxymbas Esponolas" and has sometimes been spelled Caximbas. The big shell mound at Caxambas supplied road-building material for the county, including the road to Royal Palm Hammock, which was completed in 1938. Workers loaded the shell on barges and towed it up the canal dredged beside the roadbed to Caxambas, which was later merged with the nearby community of Goodland. In 1971, the ancient Indian mound was leveled; remnants can still be seen.

Tropical Beach at Marco Island, Florida

Top: Welcome Aboard the Rosie O'Shea.
The *Rosie O'Shea*, an authentic Mississippi River paddlewheeler, was docked at O'Shea's Restaurant on Marco Island. The boat took visitors on lunch and dinner cruises around the island. *Circa 1980s, $1-3.*

Far Left: Tropical Beach at Beautiful Marco Island.
Bev and Art mailed this beach postcard to Mr. & Mrs. W. Albers in Maplewood, New Jersey: "This is a lush beach. Enjoying this life and area. Will be leaving for home Sunday. Weather perfect. Lots of fishing for Art." *Cancelled 1973, $1-3.*

Near Left: Shelling on the Beach at Marco Island.
Shells wash ashore on Marco Island in incomprehensible mounds that accumulate on the beach, causing sane people to walk around for hours in a hunched-over position collecting these colorful gifts from the sea. *Circa 1970s, $4-6.*

Prehistoric People at Key Marco

In the spring of 1895, Smithsonian archaeologist Frank Hamilton Cushing traveled to Key Marco (now Marco Island) to investigate an area where local resident William D. Collier had discovered some unusual artifacts. Collier had been digging in a mucky area for garden soil when he unearthed well-preserved wooden objects, ancient cordage, and shell tools. Cushing conducted minimal test excavations and arranged with Collier to return with a full crew for a more extensive project. The following year he returned to Marco Island on board the *Silver Spray*, a sailing schooner loaned to Cushing as an expedition headquarters. Accompanying him was Wells Moses Sawyer, expedition artist and photographer, and nine other crew members. From February through May, they labored in rough conditions to uncover the history of a culture previously unknown to scholars. The project was headline news and the finds have since become known worldwide. Cushing shipped the objects north and divided them between the sponsoring institutions: the Smithsonian and the University of Pennsylvania Museum in Philadelphia. In the 1970s, a portion of this collection was transferred from Philadelphia to the Florida Museum of Natural History in Gainesville, Florida. The eight images contained in this section are artifacts or reproductions of artifacts uncovered at the Key Marco site and are on exhibit at the Florida Museum of Natural History.

Masks from the Key Marco Site.
Calusa ceremonies involving masked processions were observed by the Spanish explorers in the sixteenth century. The masks were kept in a temple built on a mound. Many of the carved and painted masks found at the Key Marco site crumbled away after being removed from the peat. Fortunately, Wells Sawyer took photographs of the objects as they were unearthed and after they had been cleaned. Wells used these photographs to make lively watercolor paintings showing the vivid colors of the original objects. These paintings are permanent records of these priceless artifacts and a part of the National Anthropological Archives at the Smithsonian Institution in Washington, D.C. Reproductions of these famous Calusa masks are in museums throughout Florida. Ancient Hands, a company in Georgia, specializes in manufacturing museum quality reproductions of ancient Indian art works. They have excellent reproductions of the Calusa masks, many of which are sold in the Florida Museum Gift Shop.

Visitors to the Keys and Glades of Southern Florida in the late nineteenth century were often amazed at the vast deposits of shells that had been left there by prehistoric people. In some places these refuse heaps had been turned into built-up living and ceremonial areas, including Demorey's Key, where men had constructed a monumental sea wall more than ten-feet high, mostly of conch shells. Explored by Cushing in 1896, beyond the wall were terraces with a graded pathway leading to five large mounds and a big pyramidal mound that probably supported a temple.

Cushing and his expedition crew spent two months on the South Florida Gulf Coast digging in the mangrove muck on the island. From this wet site,

Painted Human Figure.
This little man painted on the valve of a clam shell may represent a dancer in costume. It is the only known human image painted by a Calusa artist. The outline sketch technique is remarkably like contemporary cartooning. Note the feathered headdress. The designs around the wrists may represent strings of beads. The shell is 3.5" high.

less than an acre in size, came an assortment of aboriginal artifacts (more than 1,000) unique in North America. The preservative properties of the muck at Key Marco were almost unbelievable. Cushing found not only objects of stone, shell, bone, and pottery, but also a wonderful array of perishables: things made of wood and fiber, held together with gum, rawhide, and twisted gut. Such artifacts are almost never preserved, but when they are, they add immeasurable to the understanding of a past culture.

Among the wooden objects found were bowls, mortars and pestles, spears and atlatls (a spear-throwing stick), and handles for a wide variety of tools. Many of the seemingly utilitarian objects were beautifully carved from hardwoods such as mangrove and lignum vitae and were smoothed and polished. The Marco Island people were fishers; their fishing technology was represented by cord, ropes, and nets made of palm fiber, net floats made from cypress pegs and gourds, and fishhooks made of wood and bone. Even more intriguing were the ceremonial objects. From the protective peat came carved clubs set with shark teeth, wooden tablets, and plaques, hardwood ear spools with polished shell rims, realistically carved animal heads, and elaborately carved and painted masks.

104

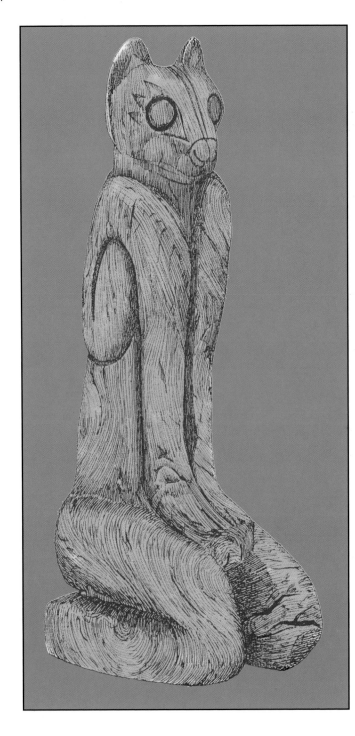

At the time Key Marco was excavated, techniques for preserving wood and other fragile materials removed from the muck had not been developed. The colors on the painted objects quickly faded, and many objects quickly deteriorated. Fortunately, a photographer with the excavation party photographed all of the objects soon after they were removed from the pond. Watercolors were also prepared showing the colors of the painted objects.

Dating the Cushing finds has been a problem. No record of the stratification of the objects was kept, so that they cannot be placed in sequence. There is no sign of European trade goods or influence in the finds. Radiocarbon dating did not exist at the time of excavation, and radiocarbon dating of objects that have been handled and stored away from their original environment for long periods may not be reliable. In the 1960s, an attempt to radiocarbon date some objects yielded a date of 1670 A.D. A second attempt in 1975, using five different objects, yielded dates from 55 A.D. to 850 A.D.

In 1896, Cushing published his findings in *The Proceedings of the American Philosophical Society, Volume 35, Number 153,* titled "Exploration of Ancient Key Dwellers' Remains on the Gulf Coast of Florida." AMS Press, Inc., of New York, published a reprint of these findings in 1975. Describing the Key Marco dwellers in the elegant prose of the nineteenth century, he wrote:

"...their art is not only an art of the sea, but is an art of shells and teeth, an art for which the sea supplied nearly all the working parts of tools, the land only some of the materials worked upon."

Today the Cushing artifacts, photographs, and sketches are housed at several different museums, including the Museum of Natural History of the Smithsonian; The University Museum, University of Pennsylvania; the Museum of the American

Cat Effigy.
This carving of a seated cat, panther, or lion resembles the famous Egyptian figure of the god Bast. Of the many artifacts of ceremonial importance—the masks, bird, and animal representations—the one that has captured the most popular attention is the cat figurine. Cushing was impressed with the detail and quality of the exquisite artwork. The carving was six inches high, 2.5 inch width at the base, carved from a hard knot, or gnarled block of fine, dark-brown wood; it had been saturated with the fat of slain animals or a type of varnish. The original cat effigy is located at the Smithsonian Institution in Washington, D.C.

Woodpecker Tablet.
The wooden tablet with an ivory-billed woodpecker (now an extinct species) painted on it is 16.5" by 8.5". The cypress wood tablet was shaved with shark tooth blades to a uniform thickness of less than half an inch. On one side is painted the figure of a crested bird, with four beads falling from its mouth; once colored blue, white, and red, they may represent speech or a call.

Indian, and the Florida Museum of Natural History in Gainesville.

The original Key Marco site was completely excavated and refilled; it's now under a housing subdivision.

The Marco Island Historical Museum features several ancient Calusa Indian artifacts that were found on the Olde Marco Island Inn, which opened in 1883 with twenty bedrooms and an outhouse on a Calusa Indian shell mound.

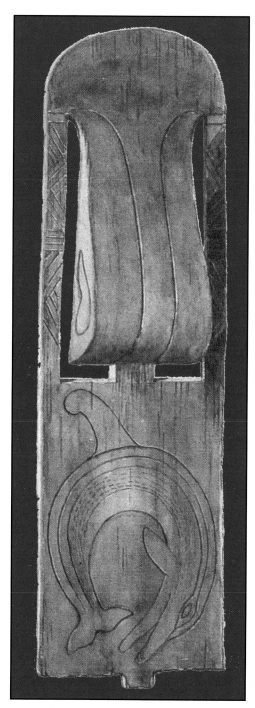

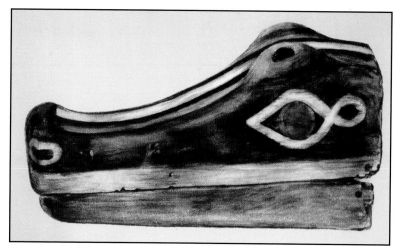

Alligator Figurine.
The alligator figurine with articulated jaws has a lower jaw approximately 9.5" long. The original is in the University Museum, University of Pennsylvania.

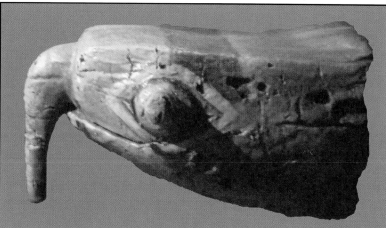

Sea Turtle Figurehead.
The beaked turtle head effigy sculpture, carved from soft wood, is approximately seven inches and is painted in black, white, blue, and red pigments. The original sea turtle effigy is located in the University Museum, University of Pennsylvania.

Decorated Wooden Amulet.
Leaping dolphin carved on a wooden amulet or tablet. Two fragments of the original tablet are in the collections of the Florida Museum of Natural History. This Wells Sawyer's watercolor painting of the tablet is part of the Calusa Indian display at the Gainesville, Florida museum.

Deer Head Effigy.
This artifact represented the finest and preserved example of combined carving and painting. The head is a young deer or doe; 7.5" in length and 5.5" in breadth across the forehead; the base of the ears were hollow and tubular. The Calusa Indian who carved this deer head made the ears movable. It dates to between 800 A.D. and 1400 A.D. The original deer artifact is in the University Museum, University of Pennsylvania.

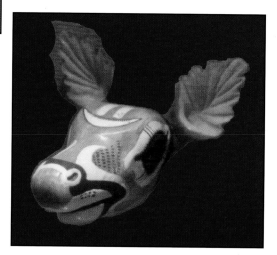

Part IV: Florida Plant Life

An Orange Grove, Florida.

Producing a Variety of Delicious Fruits.
Many northern breakfast tables draw their winter delicacies from the Florida west coast where orange, grapefruit, tangelo, tangerine, lemon, lime, and kumquat all thrive. *Circa 1915, $3-5.*

Chapter Fourteen:
Citrus

Florida's fertile soil and long days of sunshine make the state a good place to grow food. Agriculture has fueled much of Florida's economic development. Today, Florida is the nation's top producer of sugar cane and is also a leading state in the production of fresh vegetables including tomatoes, corn, beans, bell peppers, and celery.

When most people think of Florida agricultural products, they think about oranges and grapefruits. There is a good reason for this. Florida produces seventy-nine percent of the nation's citrus fruit. Grapefruit production in Florida is the largest in the world.

Citrus came to Florida by a long route. It was brought to Spain from the Orient and then to Florida by the Spanish. Christopher Columbus brought the first citrus to the New World in 1493. Early Spanish explorers planted the first orange trees around St. Augustine. Pedro Menendez, a Spanish soldier, reported abundant groves around St. Augustine in 1565. The Spanish took the plantings with them everywhere they went. By 1800 trees were growing along the St. Johns River, Tampa Bay, and St. Augustine. As the population grew and expanded to new areas, citrus trees spread also. Railroads made it possible for groves to be planted in the interior away from rivers. Growers often sold their fruit from sheds built near

IN SOUTHERN FLORIDA.

Packing Oranges.
Pioneer citrus growers first packed each box of fruit personally—washing, wrapping, and shipping. They were often called Mom & Pop Fruit Packers. Shown is an early 1900s citrus packing plant in southern Florida. In packing oranges, boxes of light material were made, and each orange was wrapped separately in tissue paper. They were placed closely together in layers, so that there would be no rolling or sliding, and care was taken that only one grade was put into each box. According to the size of the fruit, a standard box would hold from 100 to 250 oranges. *Cancelled 1917, $14-16.*

railroad stops. Markets began to open in northern cities for oranges and other citrus fruits. By 1910, citrus groves were located all over central and southern Florida, and citrus production grew steadily over the next several decades.

In 1924, there were close to 390,000 citrus trees in Lee County bearing better than 1,125,000 boxes of fruit. Fruit production the same year was 340,473 crates of oranges; 540,838 crates of grapefruit; 12,760 cases of guava, 1,692 crates of mangoes; 1,307 crates of alligator pears; 62,980 coconuts; 11,500 pounds of grapes; and 28,807 bunches of bananas.

Citrus groves once dotted much of Florida, but citrus trees are easily damaged when the temperature dips below freezing for too many hours or too many consecutive days. That is what happened to many of the citrus fields in the northern part of the state. Today, most of Florida's citrus groves are concentrated in the southern part of the state.

With the development of the railroad and steamship systems, citrus growers in Florida who had been primarily supplying a local demand had the potential to become national suppliers. To increase sales, they were now faced with the problem of packing, shipping, identifying, and advertising a product for customers who lived thousands of miles away. The colorful paper fruit crate label, which was born in California in the 1880s, with bright and eye-catching designs, was used to identify a particular citrus packer's product. The brightly printed labels were attached to the ends of the wooden slatted citrus crates. The standard crate used by Florida citrus packers had an indented end that allowed the use of a 9"x9" label. (A 6"x6" label was used on a smaller box or, in some cases, a strip label about 3"x9".) Citrus growers and packers selected and designed their own labels. In many cases, the designs used on the labels were works of art, often related to their special interests or call attention to their product in the face of hundreds of competing brands.

170. BIRD'S EYE VIEW OF AN ORANGE GROVE, FLORIDA.

Orange Grove in Blossom, Florida.

Florida Citrus Grove.
Introduced in Spanish times, oranges became a valuable Florida product early on. Pioneer growers first shipped fruit to northern markets by steamboat, steamship, and railroad. Now they are scientifically cared for, grown by the square mile, and shipped by a variety of methods. *Circa 1915, $3-5.*

Left: Picking Oranges.
Hand-picking was the only way to get citrus off the trees, and still would be, until mechanical pickers were perfected in the 1980s. Twenty- to thirty-foot ladders were common in the early years before citrus trees were hedged yearly. *Circa 1910, $4-6.*

Below: Picking Time in Sunny Florida.
Pretty girls often helped the citrus industry advertise their products. These two young lassies are helping Florida growers sell their citrus products. *Circa 1950s, $3-5.*

Grapefruit Pickers.
This mature grapefruit grove yielded about 200 to 400 boxes of grapefruit per acre. The grapefruit trees were planted sixty trees to an acres. Today, however, citrus trees are planted closer together and the fruit yield is much higher. *Circa 1907, $4-6.*

110

Alva Citrus Packing Houses.
Alva was founded in 1870 by Danish captain Peter Nelson. While sailing up the Caloosahatchee River looking for the land of his dreams, Nelson noticed angelic white flowers blanketing the river bank. The white flowers, called Alva in Danish, reminded Nelson of his home in Denmark. Nelson claimed the land as his own and laid out a set of plans, including space for churches, a school, public parks, recreation areas, and a library. In 1901, the Alva Book Club began meeting. The building that hosted these gatherings later became the first public library in Southwest Florida. The structure was eventually turned into a museum. Alva is also the location of Eden Vineyards, the oldest operating winery in Florida. Alva is located a few miles east of Fort Myers. *Circa 1930s, $20-40.*

TEDDY BRAND

DE-LIGHTFUL

PACKED BY **ALVA PACKING COMPANY, ALVA.** LEE COUNTY FLORIDA

LEOPARD Brand
REG. U.S. PAT. OFF.

PACKED BY
ALVA CITRUS GROWERS ASSN.
ALVA, LEE COUNTY, FLA.

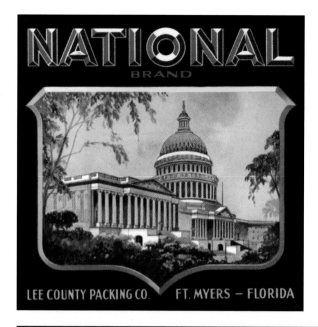

Fort Myers Citrus Crate Labels.
Early citrus crate labels (1880s–1920) were produced by stone lithography and incorporated birds, flowers, animals, and naturalistic motifs. Many of these label designs had no relation to the product advertised. About 1920 offset printing replaced lithography and label design changed, with many now emphasizing the health benefits of the citrus product. More children, animals, and "pin-up" female designs were used on labels. From about 1935 to the mid-1950s, commercial art designers steered the citrus label away from aesthetic images and more toward brand identification. Large block letters, one-word identifications, geometric shapes, and cartoon images became the order of the day. Over 5,000 separate designs were created during the era of the Florida citrus crate label. These labels decorated the fruit products of Florida from the 1900s—when the railroad network allowed for nationwide transportation of fruit—to the 1950s, when the traditional wooden crate gave way to cardboard cartons. The golden age of the citrus crate label was from the 1920s to the 1940s. *Circa 1920s-1940s, $10-$100.*

Chapter Fifteen:

Natural Wonders of Florida

In 1513, when Spanish explorer Juan Ponce de Leon first stepped onto the shores of the land he named Florida, he encountered a profusion of native plants and colorful flowers.

The soil, climate, and moisture of Florida have given it a great richness in trees, plants, and shrubs, including many that are extremely rare and exotic.

Many useful trees grow in Florida in addition to those used for timber. The Sabal or cabbage palm tree was one of the first to have its merit discovered. Possibly for this reason, as well as its beauty, it was named the state tree of Florida in 1953. Since the earliest times, the white, tender top bud, the heart of palm, has been harvested for food. This tastes more like artichoke than cabbage, but the name continues.

Mulberries, guavas, olives, avocados, and almost every other fruit or commercial tree have been tried in Florida with varying degrees of success. Eucalyptus, though not a native, grows tremendously, sometimes reaching a height of seventy feet and a thickness of twenty inches in as little as six years. Florida's most famous tree—the orange—is not a native either. Many

Above: Coconuts from Fort Myers.
To open a coconut, first remove the fibrous husk that covers the hard nut. One of the three spots is softer than the others. Puncture it and remove the coconut milk. Crack the hard shell and remove the sweet white coconut meat. The raw flesh of the coconut is used for food or, if dried, is called copra, a great source of vegetable oil. Coconut milk is used in cooking or as a beverage. *Circa 1916, $2-4.*

Right: Coconut Palms.
The coconut palm is probably one of the most versatile palms. The husk of the coconut is the source of coir used for ropes and mats. Trunks of coconut palms yield wood for constructing furniture. Palm leaves are used for baskets or roofing material. Many other uses could still be mentioned since every part of the palm is used. According to an old Indian saying, "If you take care of a coconut palm for the first seven years of its life; it will take care of you for the rest of your life." *Circa 1904, $5-7.*

A Well Dressed Coconut Picker. *Cancelled 1913, $5-7.*

Street Lined With Royal Palms.
The Florida Royal Palm is native to the cypress swamps of South Florida and likes full sun and plenty of water to look its best. There is not a more impressive palm with which to line a roadway. *Circa 1940s, $1-3.*

wild oranges found in remote areas of Florida are thought to have grown from seed dropped by early Spanish explorers.

Bald cypress trees are found throughout Florida. Mature trees have spreading branches that form an uneven rounded crown. The straight trunk usually is swollen and buttressed at the base; it may reach six to twelve feet in diameter at the bottom. In marshy areas, root outgrowths, or "knees," emerge from around the drip line of the bald cypress. These are one to four feet high, conical at first but developing into unusual shapes. Knees bring air to the roots when the soil around the tree is flooded.

Live oak, laurel oak, and water oak trees are widely found in Florida. The live oak, a giant tree of the South, is well known in Florida history. When ships were made of wood, this tree was so highly prized that in 1799 the U.S. government bought vast tracks of live oak timberland for building warships. The live oak is rarely over sixty feet tall; however, it may be three times that wide. Heavy spreading branches grow horizontally from the short, massive trunk, which may be up to six feet in diameter.

Popular palm trees in the Fort Myers area and other South Florida locations are the coconut palm and the royal palm.

The coconut palm reaches a height of fifty to one hundred feet and has a slender, arched trunk with a thick, distended base. Its graceful crown is formed by feathery leaves fifteen to twenty feet long and five feet wide. The trees bear flowers and nuts of various sizes. The unripe nut yields a sweet beverage and the meat is used as a vegetable.

The royal palm has a straight trunk and grows to a height of eighty feet. Alternate leaves are dark green, twelve to fifteen feet long. Royal palms will not withstand drought, salt, or freezing weather.

114

Mangroves are trees that grow in inter-tidal salty environments because they can tolerate frequent flooding and are able to obtain fresh water from salt water. Florida's estimated 400,000-500,000 acres of mangrove forests contribute to the overall health of the state's southern coats. People living along South Florida's coastline benefit in many ways from mangroves. In addition to providing fish habitats, mangrove forests protect uplands from storm winds, waves, and floods.

Altogether over three hundred species of trees grow in Florida. More than half of all kinds of trees found in North America (north of Mexico) are found in Florida.

Florida lives up to its reputation as a land of flowers by producing a profusion of 3,000 different varieties of flowers. Most of these are native, but many have been imported. Hibiscus, jacaranda, bird of paradise, air plants, gardenia, azalea, camellia, yellow jasmine, flame vine, roses, mimosa, chrysanthemum, snapdragon, verbena, cosmos, dahlia, zinnia, petunia, marigold, pansy, begonia, poinsettias, Spanish bayonet, and exotic foliage plants all flash their colors across the Florida scene in various seasons. Visitors who are accustomed to seeing small poinsettia plants in pots can scarcely recover from the sight of enormous "trees" covered with hundreds of enormous poinsettia blossoms. Orchids bloom wild in many Florida woods, marshes, and lowlands. The tree orchids of South Florida are larger and more impressive in their individual blooms, and there are more than twenty-five native varieties of these.

Much of the flowering shrubbery seen planted along the streets and highways is oleander. The blossoms may be red, yellow, white, or pink, and bloom nearly all the year.

The showy bougainvillea vine climbs in great profusion over trees, trellises, fences, and sides of buildings. One vine may spread a mass of brilliant pink, purple, flame, or scarlet over an area of two hundred feet.

Packing Pineapples.
Pineapple plantations were located in the Fort Myers area along the Caloosahatchee River and east of the city. *Circa 1910, $6-8.*

On the leaning trunks of live oak trees an interesting fern grows. This is the popular resurrection fern. In dry weather it shrinks into a brown dead-looking ball, but with moisture it revives into sparkling green.

Spanish moss is a grey, mossy-looking plant that hangs in long strands from trees and creates an eerie effect. An air plant that does not need soil or feed from the tree, it lives entirely on air and rain.

Florida has about 3,500 species of wildflowers, each with its own special beauty and character. Many showy species bloom profusely along the roadsides, with each season offering an array of plant colors. In the spring there are such species as blue-eyed grass, evening primroses, phlox, fleabanes, and groundsels. Autumn brings goldenrods, blazing stars and sunflowers. Florida's state parks have nature trails and boardwalks where one can view wildflowers in natural settings.

13617 Pineapple Field, Florida.

Pineapple Field.
Pineapples, fresh or canned, were shipped to northern cities as a money crop. *Cancelled 1910, $1-3.*

Cutting Bananas, Florida.

Left: Banana Trees Bearing Fruit.
Although some may reach thirty feet in height, Banana plants are not trees, but herbaceous perennials. Various kinds are found in Fort Myers; some of them cultivated for their bright flowers, others for their delicious fruit. Banana stalks die soon after fruiting, but each dying stalk is usually replaced by several new suckers. *Circa 1930s, $1-3.*

Poinsettias in Bloom, Florida

PHOTO COURTESY FLORIDA CYPRESS GARDENS

Above: Poinsettias in Bloom.
An ever increasing variety of flora flourishes luxuriantly in the soil and climate of Fort Myers. From far tropical corners of the world many exotic species have been transplanted further to beautify the landscape. The brilliant red Christmas flowers bloom most of the winter in Fort Myers and other Southwest Florida cities. *Circa 1930s, $2-4.*

Right: Sea Grape.
This multi-trunked, evergreen tree grows to about twenty feet tall. It is picturesque in the landscape and the fruit is a boon to wildlife. The leathery, nearly circular leaves are six to eight inches wide, dark green above and lighter below, with reddish veins. This sea-grape tree is on Sanibel Island. *Author photograph.*

Palm Beach, Fla. Rubber Tree in the Jungle.

Royal Poinciana Tree in Florida

Photo by Romer

Top Left: Banyan Trees.
The Banyan is one of Florida's most remarkable trees. It sprouts even from a seed dropped by a bird on the limb of some other kind of tree, as roots will descend to the soil. In time it kills the trees on which it grew. As the branches develop, they grow downward and take roots as they touch the ground. Banyan trees have been known to grow horizontal branches up to 2,000 feet. They are a magnificent evergreen—a botanical wonder! *Circa 1914, $3-5.*

Above: Rubber Tree in the Jungle.
Some roads around Fort Myers were cut through the otherwise impassible jungle; its dense bamboo thickets yielded only to the machete, wielded by vigorous arms. Here in this tropical paradise is the rubber tree, with its fantastic shapes. Here also are the bamboo, the palm, and the coconut. Spanish moss festoons the oaks and orchids hang from the branches overhead. *Circa 1907, $3-5.*

Near Left: Royal Poinciana Tree in Full Bloom.
Winter tourists staying in Fort Myers during the January-to-March season missed seeing the spectacular umbrella-shaped, semitropical Royal Poinciana tree in bloom. The regal red flowers of the Royal Poinciana, appropriately nicknamed "the flame tree," appeared in late spring and early summer. *Circa 1940s, $1-3.*

Part V: Traveling Around Southwest Florida

Crossing the Everglades.
Until the 1920s, getting from the west coast of Florida to the east coast took some doing. There was a road running from Tampa to Daytona Beach, but nothing south of there. There were some old Seminole Indian trails, and it was possible to cross from Fort Myers to Miami in less than a week if you could battle the mosquitoes, snakes, alligators, and other wildlife. *Circa 1930s, $3-5.*

Chapter Sixteen:

Tamiami Trail and Everglades

In the early days, there was no feasible means of transportation to make the area easily accessible. That is why the Tamiami Trail was so desperately needed. Unfortunately, the state had no money for the project. Barron G. Collier made a deal with the state: he would finance the building of the road through the area today known as Collier County if the state, in turn, would name a county after him. The east-west part of the Trail crosses the Florida Everglades, a remote tropical wilderness larger than the state of Delaware. This area consisted of a few widely scattered settlements and less than 1,200 people with no electric power, telephones, or telegraphs, and not a single mile of paved road.

The Tamiami Trail

Greetings from Tamiami Trail.
The Tamiami Trail starts in Tampa, crosses the Manatee River, and passes through Bradenton, Sarasota, Venice, Punta Gorda, Fort Myers, Bonita Springs, and Naples before going through the Florida Everglades toward Miami. The Trail officially opened April 25, 1928, linking Tampa to Miami via Southwest Florida. Key views on this postcard: **Upper left:** Memorial Pier Building and Yacht Basin, Bradenton; **Upper right:** Venice Street Scene; **Lower left:** Palm-lined First Street, Fort Myers; **Lower center:** Sarasota Lido; **Lower right:** Punta Gorda Bridge. *Circa 1930s, $3-5.*

The famed Tamiami Trail is named for its terminal cities, Tampa and Miami. It's the highway that connects the Atlantic Ocean with the Gulf of Mexico, proceeding in long straight stretches across the Everglades, a primeval swampland. The highway also connects Fort Myers, Bonita Springs, and Naples with other cities along the Gulf Coast.

Tamiami Trail Trivia

- The Tamiami Trail passes through seven counties. The longest and toughest stretch—seventy-six miles (28%) of the road—was built across Collier County.

- A bonus system sped up road construction from .7 miles to 1.1 miles per month; the record was two miles built in a month.

- Despite the heat, seven-foot-long rattlesnakes, and hazardous conditions, no lives were lost building the trail across Collier County.

- Explosives had to be hauled in by oxen. In rough spots men shouldered the boxes of dynamite themselves and floundered neck-deep in water.

- Giant dredges followed the dynamiters, throwing up huge piles of rock from the canal created by the dredges.

- The 31-mile stretch from Carnestown to the Dade County line had to be blasted out of solid limerock and piled up again to form the roadbed.

- Seminole Indians proved invaluable as guides and were given free bus fare on the Trail until World War II.

- There have been reports of a 300-pound brown bear and Florida panther engaging motorists' automobiles.

- The average Trail worker earned about 20¢ per hour and literally lived on the job in portable bunkhouses complete with cooks and rolling kitchens.

- The Seminole Indians built small shelters along the route where food could be stored to help travelers.

- Reports that work crews had struck quicksand in January 1925 sparked fears for a time that the road project would be abandoned.

- Work on the Tamiami Trail alone used up a railroad boxcar of dynamite every three weeks for three years.

- The Trail's first traffic accident occurred just hours after the road was officially opened when a dozy driver fell asleep at the wheel and flipped his car over.

- Sawmills and logging camps provided the lumber needed for buildings and bridges.

- The official flag of the Tamiami Trail is red with a white band running diagonally across, and the Trail insignia in the center.

- During the 1930s and 1940s many Seminole Indian villages were built along the Trail.

- Occasional service stations dot the Trail at sufficient intervals to meet all requirements of the average motorist.

The idea for building a highway (the Tamiami Trail) to connect Florida's East and West coasts originated in 1915 with Dade County's tax assessor, Captain J. F. Jaudon, and in 1916, he completed surveys of the route. Construction began in 1917, but proceeded slowly because of labor shortage during World War I. In 1923, a motorcade traveled over the proposed route to arouse public interest. The trail-blazing expedition of ten cars, twenty-three men, and two Indian guides, left Fort Myers on April 4, 1923. After a perilous three-week trip, seven cars reached Miami, and the trail became the most discussed highway project in America. Smoothed and surfaced, the road was opened to traffic on April 25, 1928 at a cost of $13,000,000. An immediate success, the highway helped to unite the lower East and West coasts of Florida. What once involved a two-day roundabout journey by automobile was now accomplished in little more than two hours.

Along the north side of the road runs the Tamiami Canal, a long ditch from which rock and mulch were taken to build the elevated roadbed. The canal side of the road is alive with birds, reptiles, and fish. Sometimes raccoons, rabbits, turtles, alligators, and cottonmouth moccasin snakes can be seen.

Keeper of the Everglades.
East along the Tamiami Trail (U.S. Highway 41) from Naples is found what Marjory Stoneman Douglas, Florida's most respected conservationist, describes as the great "river of grass"—the Everglades. This unusual subtropical ecosystem rally is a vast slow-moving shallow river that once covered the entire southern tip of Florida. Over two million acres have been preserved here for the pleasure of alligators, birds, fish, and people who enjoy them. The Everglades is the New York City of Florida's alligator population. They thrive in the freshwater ponds and brackish creeks of the "river of grass." *Circa 1940, $2-4.*

Many Seminole Indian villages were scattered along the trail between Miami and Naples, hidden from view behind palisaded walls, above which rise the sun-bleached palmetto thatched roofs of the native houses. In front of each village was a shop in which Seminole Indian jackets, dresses, dolls, metal pins and buttons, air plants, miniature boats, postcards, and other native products were sold. Seminole women used hand-operated sewing machines to produce many of the souvenir products.

The completion of the Tamiami Trail across the Everglades opened isolated Seminole Indian camps to the rapid tourist development of Southwest Florida.

Today the Tamiami Trail is the southernmost 275 miles of U.S. Highway 41 from State Road 60 in Tampa to U.S. Highway 1 in Miami. The 165-mile north-south section extends to Naples, whereupon it becomes an east-west road crossing the Everglades before reaching Miami. The Tamiami Trail has been designated a National Scenic Byway by the United States Department of Transportation for its unique scenery in the Everglades and the Big Cypress Swamp.

The Everglades

The Everglades, a shallow fifty-mile "river of grass," is a vast, complex water system that flows from Lake Okeechobee south more than one hundred miles to Florida Bay. Its 4.3 million acres contains a unique ecosystem of remarkable plants and animals found nowhere else on earth. Hundreds of alligators can often be seen at Shark Valley in Everglades National Park. At Shark Valley, located on U.S. Highway 41 (Tamiami Trail) west of Miami, Park Rangers operate a fifteen-mile loop tram ride in the Everglades. The burrow pits at the observation tower are hangouts for alligators. The tower provides an opportunity to get more of a bird's-eye view and a better understanding of the Everglades landscape.

ROSEATE SPOONBILLS IN THE EVERGLADES

The landscape of the Everglades is as flat as a tabletop. Its highest point is only twenty-five feet above sea level. From Lake Okeechobee, it tilts very slightly to the southwest, toward the Gulf of Mexico. The Everglades are based on limerock that was once under the sea. The rock is filled with fossils of ancient sea creatures. In many parts of the Everglades, the rock is covered by peat, the remains of plants that partially decayed ages ago. The heart of the Everglades is a region of vast, flooded prairies, covered with tall sedge called saw grass. The saw grass in the Everglades grows tall, often elven feet or more.

Animal life in the Everglades is a mixture. More than two hundred species of fish have been found in Everglades' waters. More than three hundred species of birds rest on tree limbs, paddle in the water and fly overhead. More than forty species of mammals inhabit the great marsh. Among the rarest is the Florida panther. Other animals in the Everglades include deer, black bears, raccoons, rats, turtles, and snakes.

In the Everglades, however, the alligator is king. Thousands of gators live in the saw grass prairies, in the sloughs, and in culverts that pass under dirt roads in parts of the Everglades National Park.

The alligator has earned the title of "keeper of the Everglades." It cleans out the large holes dissolved in the Everglades' limestone bed and these functions as oasis in the dry winter season. Fish, turtles, snails, and other fresh water animals seek refuge in these life-rich solution holes, which become feeding grounds for alligators, birds, and mammals until the rains return. Survivors, both predators and prey, then leave the holes to repopulate the Everglades.

To the south, the Florida Everglades extend all the way to Cape Sable and the mangrove islands at the spear-like tip of the peninsula. Beyond eye range of the visitor are vast areas strewn with the white skeletons of trees, torn and twisted by the power of the winds, and thousands of islands and wide prairies seeming more like a part of the South American pampas than a section of America. The Everglades stretch all the way to Lake Okeechobee, Florida's inland sea. The prairies are low, sandy, grassy, and comparatively treeless tracts.

The human inhabitants of the interior of South Florida blend with its untamed atmosphere, for the Seminole Indians are the only American Indians who have never, since the end of hostilities, signed a formal treaty with the United States Government. They constitute an independent remnant of a tribe that fought the United States Army in two of the most furiously contested wars ever waged by Indians.

"Boo louder," said Marjory Stoneman Douglas to her jeering opponents during a 1970 debate on the fate of the Everglades marshlands. And they did. Known as the "Grandmother of the Glades," Douglas, then in her eighties, was no stranger to hostile receptions. She was, once again, fighting to save her beloved Everglades from destruction. Where critics saw a "wholly valueless" swamp, Douglas saw a unique river, fifty miles wide and six inches deep. Her landmark 1947 book, *The Everglades: River of Grass*, linked her name with a passionate movement to preserve the region and its wildlife long before ecology became a household word.

Everglades National Park.
With an entrance twenty-eight miles southeast of Naples, Everglades is the third-largest national park in the United States. A 1.5 million-acre expanse of grassy river, it's the perfect place for nature photographers, bird watchers, and visitors who want to witness Florida wildlife. The Everglades is one of the most challenged ecosystems in the United States. Its subtropical wilderness is home to a dozen endangered creatures including the Florida panther, the snail kite, the wood stork, the American crocodile, and the West Indian manatee. Everglades National Park was dedicated December 6, 1947. President Harry S. Truman said: "Here are no lofty peaks seeking the sky, no might glaciers or rushing streams wearing away the uplifted land. Here is land, tranquil in its quiet beauty, serving not as a source of water but as a last receiver of it." *Circa 1940s, $1-3.*

The Seminole Indians

The Seminole Indians are not native to Florida. They migrated here in the middle of the eighteenth century, long after the Spaniards had discovered and settled this part of America. At first they made their home in the more fertile regions of northern Florida, but when the United States took over the government of Florida, they were forced to retreat further into the interior until finally only the forbidding wilderness of the Everglades and the Cypress Swamp lay open to them. Today, Florida's Seminole Indians live in established Indian reservations and several Indian villages. The Seminoles ideas of dress, justice, and behavior have changed little through the years.

Seminole Indians Along the Trail

During the 1930s and 1940s many Seminole Indians living in the Everglades moved to and built their villages and camps along this modern highway. In roadside stands and concessions, they displayed their handicraft products; dolls, handbags, beautifully designed jackets, capes, and dresses were all for sale to tourists.

Almost every Seminole Indian camp along the Tamiami Trail was a sightseeing concession where, for an admission fee, the tourist could enter and inspect the village. As an added attraction, a high-walled pen of alligators was shown nearby. Permission was usually granted for tourists to taking snapshots, but generally the Indians remained aloof from the visitors. Reserved and quiet, they spoke only when directly addressed. Only after many visits could a white man expect to win their confidence and friendship.

A few of the Seminole Indian families owned land. For the most part, the Seminoles along the Tamiami Trail were squatters, literally and legally. They were subject to eviction anytime at the whim of the landowner, but the nature of the property was such that few owners ever evoked such rights.

Many other Seminoles lived in isolated camps in the Everglades, far removed from the Trail or other highways. These Indians had less contact with the outside, but they did visit with other clan members living on reservations and along the Tamiami Trail.

Smallest Post Office in America

The nation's smallest post office operates out of a former 8'4" by 7'3" tomato farm tool shed on the Tamiami Trail in Ochopee. It is so tiny that no more than four people can squeeze inside at the same time! It is located thirty-five miles east of Naples and seventy miles west of Miami. Three people pick up their mail at this tiny post office situated smack dab in the middle of the Everglades. The post office is listed in the 1975 edition of a "Ripley's Believe It Or Not" book.

The white, wooden building has served as Ochopee's post office and a Trailways bus ticket office since 1953 when the former Ochopee post office, also a general store, burned. It's a tough little structure, surviving Hurricane Donna in 1960 and Hurricane Andrew in 1992, two of the country's most disastrous storms. About three hundred residents in a three-county area, mostly Indians, live in the post office's zip code, and their mail is delivered from this post office.

America's Smallest Post Office.
Cancelled 1961, $4-6.

Near Right: Seminole Indian Family in the Everglades.
The sender of this card wrote: "I have seen several families of this kind and they are sure peculiar in their habits and customs. The young girls will not talk to anyone outside of their tribe. I am told." *Cancelled 1926, $8-10.*

Far Right: Seminole Indian Village in the Everglades.
Seminole Indians have lived in the Everglades for many years. They used dugout canoes to contact other villages in the vast Everglades area. They lived in Chickees, raised wooden platforms with thatched roofs. Many of the villages located on the Trail opened their villages and sold souvenirs to tourists. *Circa 1920s, $4-6.*

Seminole Indian Family as They Live in Florida Everglades, Florida.

M19   A SEMINOLE INDIAN VILLAGE IN THE FLORIDA EVERGLADES

SCENE ALONG THE TAMIAMI TRAIL   PHOTO BY CHARLES C. EBBETS

Chapter Sixteen:

Here and There

North Fort Myers.
The City of North Fort Myers, located northwest of downtown Fort Myers, across the Caloosahatchee River, is noted for the Shell Factory and Nature Park. This sixty-year-old Shell Factory has the largest collection in the world of sea shells, fossils, coral, and other sea life specimens. The attraction offers other nautical-inspired decorations, a nature park, and a variety of retail shops. *Circa 1999, $1-3.*

Cape Coral Business District.
Fifty years ago, there was not even a small village at the modern-day site of Cape Coral. Today, located northwest of Fort Myers, across the Caloosahatchee River, it is the largest city on the river. Cape Coral is the product of a development company, which promoted the town as a "planned city" beginning in 1954. *Circa 1960s, $3-5.*

Greetings from Gatorama.
Gatorama, located on Highway 27 in Palmdale, is one of Florida's first roadside alligator attractions and reminds one of a tropical jungle. About 3,000 alligators and 250 crocodiles lurk about in this out-of-the-way property a few miles east of Fort Myers. Giant oak trees and palm trees cover the fifteen-acre attraction. Monkeys, bobcats, raccoons, peacocks, ducks, and geese also call Gatorama home. In addition to being a tourist attraction, Gatorama is an operating alligator farm and is the largest captive breeder in North America of the Acutus Crocodile.

The star attraction at Gatorama is Goliath, a fourteen-foot, forty-year-old crocodile. Goliath is the largest American crocodile in the state. Other boarders at Gatorama are Salty, a fourteen-foot saltwater crocodile; and Rambo and Mighty Mike, both thirteen-foot long gators. The highlight of any alligator roadside attraction is the feeding of the gators, and Gatorama is no exception. Chickens and pork ribs are fed to gators two times a day. The hungry mouths go through 16,000 pounds of meat a month. *Circa 2005, $1-3.*

Gatorama.
Cecil Clemons was the owner-operator of Gatorama when he produced this Gatorama postcard. *Circa 1959, $4-6.*

Immokalee.
Immokalee lies north of the Everglades a few miles southeast of Fort Myers. This agricultural community swells in population from October to May due to an influx of immigrant farmers of eight ethnicities. During these months, the town's fields are bountiful with produce, including melons, potatoes, pepper, tomatoes, and squash. On March 10, 1994 the Seminole Indian Casino opened on Indian Reservation land in Immokalee. This 47,000-square-foot gaming facility offers a variety of entertainment, from bingo, video gaming machines and poker, to fine dining at its continental dining room. The facility has around seven hundred slot machines and about two dozen poker tables. *Author photograph.*

Bibliography and Suggested Reading

Albin, Michele Wehrwein. *The Florida Life of Thomas Edison*. Gainesville, Florida: University Press of Florida, 2008.

Anholt, Betty. *Sanibel's Story: Voices and Images*. Virginia Beach, Virginia: Donning Company/Publishers, 1998.

Arnold, Kathy and Paul Wade. *The National Geographic Traveler: Florida*. Washington, D. C.: National Geographic Society, 1999.

Barnes, Alberta Colcord and Nell Colcord Weidenbach. *Early Fort Myers: Tales of Two Sisters*. Fort Myers, Florida: Self-published, 1993.

Board, Prudy Taylor. *Remembering Fort Myers: The City of Palms*. Charleston, South Carolina: The History Press, 2006.

Board, Prudy Taylor and Esther B. Colcord. *History of Ft. Myers*. Virginia Beach, Virginia: Donning Company/Publishers, 1992.

Board, Prudy Taylor and Patricia Pope Bartlett. *Lee County: A Pictorial History*. Virginia Beach, Virginia: Donning Company/Publishers, 1990.

Boone, Floyd Edward. *Boone's Florida Historical Markers and Sites*. Moore Haven, Florida: Rainbow Books, 1988.

Braden, Susan R. *The Architecture of Leisure*. Gainesville, Florida: University Press of Florida, 2002.

Brooks, Priscilla and Caroline Crabtree. *St. James City: The Early Years*. Self-published, 1982.

Brown, Barrett and Adelaide Brown. *A Short Story of Fort Myers Beach: Estero and San Carlos Islands, Florida*. Fort Myers Beach, Florida: Estero Island Publishers, 1965.

Brown, Robin C. *Florida's First People*. Sarasota, Florida: Pineapple Press, Inc., 1994.

Brown, Virginia Pounds and Laurella Owens. *The Wonderful World of the Southern Indians*. Leeds, Alabama: Beechwood Books, 1983.

Bullen, Adelaide K. *Florida Indians of Past and Present*. Gainesville, Florida: Kendall Books, 1965.

Butko, Brian and Sarah. *Roadside Attractions*. Mechanicsburg, Pennsylvania: Stackpole Books, 2007.

Campbell, George R. *The Nature of Things on Sanibel*. Sarasota, Florida: Pineapple Press, Inc., 1988.

Images of Sanibel, Captiva, Fort Myers. Fort Myers, Florida: West Summit Press, 1995.

Sanibel and Captiva: Enchanting Islands. Chagrin Falls, Ohio: West Summit Press, 1977.

Collier County Historical Society. *Naples-Marco Island*. Baton Rouge, Louisiana: Moran Publishing Corporation, 1981.

Cooley, George R. *The Vegetation of Sanibel Island*. Sanibel, Florida: Sanibel-Captiva Conservation Foundation, 1955.

Cushing, Frank Hamilton. *Exploration of Ancient Key Dwellers' Remains on the Gulf Coast of Florida*. New York, New York: AMS Press, Inc., 1973.

Damkohler, E. E. *Estero, Fla., 1882: Memoirs of the First Settler*. Fort Myers Beach, Florida: Island Press, 1967.

Dormer, Elinore M. *The Calusa: Sanibel-Captiva's Native Indians*. Sanibel Island, Florida: Sanibel-Captiva Conservation Foundation, 1981.

The Sea Shell Islands: A History of Sanibel and Captiva. Tallahassee, Florida: Rose Printing Company, 1987.

Dunn, Hampton. *Florida Sketches*. Miami, Florida: E. A. Seemann Publishing, Inc., 1974.

El Nabli, Dina. *Henry Ford: Putting The World On Wheels*. New York, New York: Harper Collins Publishers, 2008.

Firestone, Linda and Whit Morse. *A Visitor's Guide to Florida's Enchanting Islands Sanibel & Captiva*. Richmond, Virginia: Good Life Publications, 1976.

Sanibel & Captiva. Chesterfield, Virginia: Good Life Publishers, 1980.

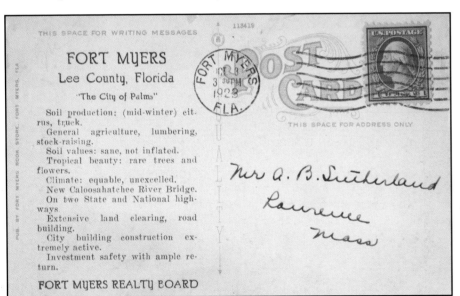

Frazer, Lynne Howard. *Naples*. Charleston, South Carolina: Arcadia Publishing, 2004.

Frisbie, Louis K. *Florida's Fabled Inns*. Bartow, Florida: Imperial Publishing Company, 1980.

Fritz, Florence. *The Unknown Story of World Famous Sanibel & Captiva*. Parsons, West Virginia: McClain Printing Company, 1974.

Unknown Florida. Coral Gables: University of Miami Press, 1963.

Garbarino, Merwyn S. *The Seminole*. New York, New York: Chelsea House Publishers, 1989.

Gibson, Charles Dana. *Boca Grande: A Series of Historical Essays*. Self-published, 1982.

Gilliland, Marion Spjut. *Key Marco's Buried Treasure*. Gainesville, Florida: University of Florida Press, 1989.

The Material Culture of Key Marco, Florida. Port Salerno, Florida: Florida Classic Library, 1989.

Greenberg, Margaret H. *Nature on Sanibel*. Ocoee, Florida: Anna Publishing, Inc., 1985.

Grismer, Karl H. *The Story of Fort Myers*. Fort Myers Beach, Florida: Island Press Publishers, 1982.

Gunderson, Ross W. *The Seashells of Sanibel and Captiva Islands*. Kenosha, Wisconsin: Self-Published, 1998.

Hann, John H., editor. *Missions to the Calusa*. Gainesville, Florida: University of Florida Press, 1991.

Hill, Yvonne and Marguerite Jordan. *Sanibel Island*. Charleston, South Carolina: Arcadia Publishing, 2008.

Hoeckel, Marilyn and Theodore B. VanItallie. *Boca Grande*. Charleston, South Carolina: Arcadia Publishing, 2000.

Hollis, Tim. *Selling The Sunshine State*. Gainesville, Florida: University Press of Florida, 2008.

Hooper, Joan S., editor. *The Best of Sanibel and Captiva Islands*. Sanibel Island, Florida: Landmark Publications, 1991.

Hudson, L. Frank. *Florida Treasure Wrecks*. Publisher and date unknown.

Hunt, Bruce. *Florida Then & Now*. Englewood, Colorado: Westcliffe Publishers, 2007.

Hutchinson, Dale I. *Bioarchaeology of the Florida Gulf Coast*. Gainesville, Florida: University Press of Florida, 2004.

Indians of the Gulf Coast States. U. S. Bureau of Indian Affairs, publishing date unknown.

Island Reporter. *A Sanibel & Captiva Family Album: A Pictorial History of the Islands*. Marceline, Missouri: Heritage House Publishing, 2003.

Jordan, Elaine Blohm. *Pine Island, the Forgotten Island*. Pine Island, Florida: Self-published, 1982.

Tales of Pine Island. Ellijay, Georgia: Jordan Ink Publishing Company, 1985.

Kaserman, James F. *Gasparilla: Pirate Genius*. Fort Myers, Florida: Pirate Publishing International, 2000.

Kozuch, Laura. *Sharks and Shark Product in Prehistoric South Florida*. Gainesville, Florida: Florida Museum of Natural History, 1993.

Lamme, Vernon. *Florida Lore Not Found in the History Books!* Boynton Beach, Florida: Star Publishing Company, 1973.

Lamoreaux, Leroy. *Early Days on Estero Island: An Old Timer Reminisces*. Fort Myers Beach, Florida: Estero Island Publishers, 1967.

Linstrom, Barbara, editor. *Sanibel-Captiva Conservation Foundation: A Natural Course*. Sanibel, Florida: Sanibel-Captiva Conservation Foundation, 2004.

Lotz, Aileen Roberts. *The City of Sanibel*. Grand Junction, Colorado: Self-published, 1999.

Ludwig, Dale. *Useppa: A Passage In Time*. Osprey, Florida: Passages Press, 2006.

MacMahon, Darcie A. and William H. Marquardt. *The Calusa and Their Legacy: South Florida People and Their Environment*. Gainesville, Florida: University Press of Florida, 2004.

Marquardt, William H., editor. *The Archaeology of Useppa Island*. Gainesville, Florida: Florida Museum of Natural History, 1999.

Martell, Scott. *Island Journeys*. Sanibel, Florida: Island Graphics, 1986.

Matthew, Jean. *We Never Wore Shoes: Growing Up On Ft. Myers Beach*. Fort Myers, Florida: Shoeless Publishing Co., 1994.

McCarthy, Kevin M. *Native Americans in Florida*. Sarasota, Florida: Pineapple Press, Inc., 1999.

Twenty Florida Pirates. Sarasota, Florida: Pineapple Press, Inc., 1994.

McGoun, William E. *Prehistoric Peoples of South Florida*. Tuscaloosa, Alabama: University of Alabama Press, 1993.

Milanich, Jerald T. and Charles H. Fairbanks. *Florida Archaeology*. Orlando, Florida: Academic Press, Inc., 1980.

Archaeology of Precolumbian Florida. Gainesville, Florida: University Press of Florida, 1994.

Florida Indians from Ancient Times to the Present. Gainesville, Florida: University Press of Florida, 1998.

Morris, Theodore. *Florida's Lost Tribes*. Gainesville, Florida: University Press of Florida, 2004.

Naples, Florida: A Photographic Portrait. Rockport, Massachusetts: Twin Lights Publishers, 2000.

Neal, Julie and Mike Neal. *Sanibel & Captiva: A Guide to the Islands*. Sanibel, Florida: Coconut Press, 2003.

Neill, Wilfred T. *The Story of Florida's Seminole Indians*. St. Petersburg, Florida: Great Outdoors, 1956.

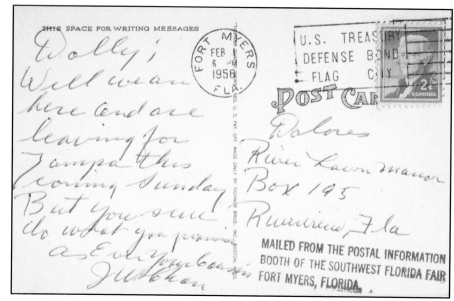

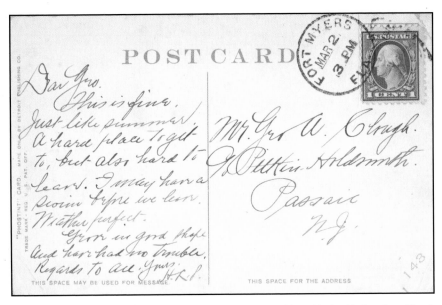

Nies, Judith. *Native American History*. New York, New York: Ballantine Books, 1996.

Nutting, E. P. *The Beginnings of Bonita Springs, Florida*. Bonita Springs, Florida: Bonita Springs Historical Society, 1986.

Peithmann, Irvin M. *The Unconquered Seminole Indians*. St. Petersburg, Florida: Great Outdoors Publishing Company, 1957.

Perry, I Mac. *Indian Mounds You Can Visit*. St. Petersburg, Florida: Great Outdoors Publishing Company, 1993.

Pinkas, Lilly. *Guide to the Gardens of Florida*. Sarasota, Florida: Pineapple Press, Inc., 1998.

Purdy, Barbara A. *Indian Art of Ancient Florida*. Gainesville, Florida: University Press of Florida, 1996.
  The Art and Archaeology of Florida's Wetlands. Boca Raton, Florida: CRC Press, 1991.

Quesnell, Quentin. *Early Estero*. Estero, Florida: Estero Historical Society, 2002.

Reaves, Gerri. *Fort Myers: Then & Now*. Charleston, South Carolina: Arcadia Publishing, 2007.

Reynolds, Charles B. *Florida Standard Guide*. New York, New York: Foster & Reynolds Company, 1927.

Sanibel and Captiva Islands. Naples, Florida: Yourtown Books, 2001.

Sanson, Nanette S. *In Portrait: Naples and Collier County*. Naples, Florida: Profolio Multimedia, Publishers, 1995.

Schell, Rolfe F. *History of Fort Myers Beach, Florida*. Fort Myers Beach, Florida: Island Press, 1980.
  1000 years on Mound Key. Fort Myers Beach, Florida: The Island Press, 1962.

Shrady, Theodore and Arthur M. Waldrop. *Orange Blossom Special: Florida's Distinguished Winter Train*. Valrico, Florida: Atlantic Coast Line and Seaboard Air Line Railroads Historical Society, 2000.

Siekman, Lula. *Handbook of Florida Shells*. St. Petersburg, Florida: Great Outdoors Association, 1957.

Sinclair, Mick. *Drive Around Florida*. Peterborough, United Kingdom: Thomas Cook Publishing, 2005.

Smith, Buckingham. *Memoir of Do d'Escalante Fontaneda Respecting Florida*. Coral Gables, Florida: Glade House, 1945.

Smoot, Tom. *The Edisons of Fort Myers*. Sarasota, Florida: Pineapple Press, 2004.

Stevens, Art. *Sanibel Shell Shocked*. New York, New York: Mercury Press, 1992.

Stewart, Laura and Susanne Hupp. *Florida Historic Homes*. Orlando, Florida: Sentinel Communications Company, 1988.

Stone, Lynn. *Sanibel Island*. Stillwater, Minnesota: Voyageur Press, 1991.

Summerlin, Cathy and Vernon Summerlin. *Traveling Florida*. Winston-Salem, North Carolina: John F. Blair, Publisher, 2002.

Tamiami Trail. Naples, Florida: Collier County Museum, date unknown.

Tebeau, Charlton W. *Florida's Last Frontier: The History of Collier County*. Coral Gables, Florida: University of Miami Press, 1957.
  They Lived in the Park. Coral Gables, Florida: University of Miami Press, 1963.

The Florida Anthropologist, Vol, 49, No. 1. Tampa, Florida: Florida Anthropological Society, 1996.

Turner, Gregg. *Fort Myers in Vintage Postcards*. Charleston, South Carolina: Arcadia Publishing, 2005.
  A Journey Into Florida Railroad History. Gainesville, Florida: University Press of Florida, 2008.

Turner, Gregg and Stan Mulford. *Ft. Myers*. Charleston, South Carolina: Arcadia Publishing, 2000.

Tuttle, Louise Carr. *Homes of Old Captiva: A Photographic Record 1900-1940*. Self-published, date unknown.

Tyrer, Jill. *J. N. "Ding" Darling National Wildlife Refuge*. Lawrenceburg, Indiana: R. L. Ruehrwein, Publisher, 2002.

Voegelin, Byron D. *South Florida's Vanished People: Travels in the Homeland of the Ancient Calusa*. Fort Myers Beach, Florida: Island Press, 1977

Walton, Chelle Koster. *The Sarasota, Sanibel Island & Naples Book*. Woodstock, Vermont: The Countryman Press, 2005.
  Florida Island Hopping: The West Coast. Sarasota, Florida: Pineapple Press, 1995.

Wheeler, Ryan J. *Treasure of the Calusa*. Tallahassee, Florida: Rose Printing, Inc., 2000.

Wilson, Charles J. *The Indian Presence: Archeology of Sanibel, Captiva and Adjacent Islands in Pine Island Sound*. Sanibel Island, Florida: Sanibel-Captiva Conservation Foundation, 1982.

Wilson, Joan Dunlop. *Pine Island Life: People and Places*. Self-published, 1986.

Wilson, John Harold and Brenda Wilson Jerman. *Beachcombing on Sanibel*. Sanibel Island, Florida: Brenda Wilson Jerman, 1978.

Winn, Ed. *Florida's Great King: King Carlos of the Calusa Indians*. Winn Publishing, 2003.

Wright, Sarah Bird. *Islands of the South and Southeastern United States*. Atlanta, Georgia: Peachtree Publishers, Ltd., 1989.

Young, Clairborne S. *Cruising Guide to Western Florida*. Gretna, Louisiana: Pelican Publishing Company, 2000.

Index